The Historical Verdicts: Pivotal Court Cases Through History

Shah Rukh

Published by Shah Rukh, 2024.

While every precaution has been taken in the preparation of this book, the publisher assumes no responsibility for errors or omissions, or for damages resulting from the use of the information contained herein.

THE HISTORICAL VERDICTS: PIVOTAL COURT CASES THROUGH HISTORY

First edition. July 28, 2024.

Written by Shah Rukh.

Table of Contents

Prologue

The pursuit of justice has been a cornerstone of human civilization, shaping societies and influencing the course of history. From the ancient tribunals of Athens to the modern courtrooms of the 21st century, landmark trials have served as pivotal moments where legal principles, societal values, and human destinies intersect. "The Historical Verdicts: Pivotal Court Cases Through History" embarks on a journey through time, exploring fifty of the most consequential and compelling court cases that have left an indelible mark on our world.

Each chapter of this book delves into a unique and renowned case, offering a window into the past where the scales of justice were weighed and fates were decided. These cases are not merely historical footnotes; they are stories of human drama, ethical dilemmas, and societal change. They illuminate the struggles between power and principle, freedom and tyranny, innovation and tradition.

From the trial of Socrates, where the foundations of Western philosophy were challenged, to the legal battles over civil rights in the 20th century, these cases reflect the evolving nature of justice and the enduring quest for truth. We witness the courage of individuals who stood against oppression, the complexities of legal arguments that shaped societal norms, and the profound impact of verdicts that resonated far beyond the courtroom walls.

In these pages, you will encounter trials that tested the limits of free speech, religious freedom, and scientific inquiry. You will see how the law has grappled with issues of morality, identity, and human rights. Each case is a testament to the enduring power of the legal system to influence hearts and minds, to bring about reform, and sometimes, to deliver profound injustice.

As we explore these historical verdicts, we are reminded that the pursuit of justice is a continuous journey. The cases presented here offer valuable lessons, cautionary tales, and moments of inspiration. They remind us of the importance of vigilance in protecting our rights and freedoms and the need for a legal system that upholds the principles of fairness and equity.

Join us as we traverse the annals of history, examining the trials that have defined eras, challenged conventions, and sparked revolutions. "The Historical Verdicts: Pivotal Court Cases Through History" invites you to reflect on the enduring impact of these landmark decisions and to consider how the lessons of the past can inform our pursuit of justice in the present and future.

Chapter 1: The Trial of Socrates

The Trial of Socrates, one of the most significant events in Western philosophical and legal history, occurred in 399 BCE in ancient Athens. This trial was not just a pivotal moment in the life of Socrates, a renowned philosopher, but also a critical reflection of the political and social climate of Athens at the time. Socrates was charged with two main accusations: corrupting the youth of Athens and impiety, specifically, introducing new gods and rejecting the traditional gods of the city. These charges were brought against him by three accusers: Meletus, a young poet; Anytus, a powerful politician; and Lycon, a rhetorician. The trial was held before a jury of 501 Athenian citizens, a typical practice in Athenian democracy, where such juries were large to prevent bribery and corruption.

Socrates' trial has been immortalized through the works of his disciples, especially Plato, who recorded the proceedings in a series of dialogues, notably "Apology," "Crito," and "Phaedo." These dialogues provide not only a philosophical exposition but also a dramatic account of the trial and its aftermath. In "Apology," Socrates delivers his defense, which is not a conventional legal argument but rather a profound reflection on his life's work and philosophy. He argues that he has been a benefactor to the city by encouraging critical thinking and moral integrity. Socrates asserts that his role as a social gadfly, constantly questioning and challenging the status quo, is a divine mission. He famously states that "the unexamined life is not worth living," emphasizing the importance of self-examination and the pursuit of truth.

The charge of corrupting the youth stems from Socrates' practice of engaging young Athenians in dialogue, encouraging them to question established norms and beliefs. His method, known as the Socratic method, involved asking probing questions to stimulate critical thinking and expose contradictions in his interlocutors' beliefs. This approach, while intellectually stimulating, also caused unease among some citizens and political leaders, who feared that it undermined traditional values and authority. The accusation of impiety was rooted in Socrates' questioning of the traditional pantheon of gods worshiped in Athens. While Socrates did not outright deny the existence of the gods, he often spoke of a singular divine voice or daimonion that guided his actions. This unconventional belief system, coupled with his criticism of the popular understanding of the gods, led to the perception that he was introducing new deities and disrespecting the traditional religious practices of Athens.

The trial's outcome was a foregone conclusion for many, given the political and social context of the time. Athens had recently undergone significant turmoil, including the Peloponnesian War, the oligarchic coup of the Thirty Tyrants, and the subsequent restoration of democracy. The instability and political tensions made Socrates, with his association with controversial figures and his challenging of authority, an easy target. The jury found Socrates guilty, and the penalty phase of the trial followed. In Athenian legal practice, both the prosecution and the defense could propose penalties, and the jury would choose between them. The prosecution demanded the death penalty. Socrates, in a provocative move, suggested that he should be rewarded for his service to the state with free meals for life, a privilege given to Olympic victors. He then offered a token fine, which was increased when his friends, including Plato, offered to contribute. However, this offer was perceived as insincere and dismissive of the seriousness of the charges, further alienating the jury.

Ultimately, the jury sentenced Socrates to death by drinking a cup of poison hemlock, a common method of execution in Athens. The sentence was carried out, and Socrates faced his death with equanimity, as described in Plato's "Phaedo." In this dialogue, Socrates engages in a final discussion on the immortality of the soul, demonstrating his commitment to philosophy and his belief in the afterlife. The trial and death of Socrates had profound implications for the future of philosophy and the perception of justice. It highlighted the tension between individual conscience and state authority, a theme that has resonated throughout history in various contexts. Socrates became a martyr for free thought and the philosophical life, inspiring subsequent generations of philosophers. His trial also raised important questions about the nature of democracy and justice, particularly the potential for majority rule to be swayed by passion and prejudice rather than reason and fairness.

Plato's portrayal of the trial and Socrates' defense has been subject to extensive interpretation and debate. Some scholars view Socrates as a tragic hero who was unjustly condemned for his pursuit of truth. Others see him as a provocateur who deliberately courted controversy and martyrdom. The historical accuracy of Plato's account is also debated, as it is colored by his admiration for Socrates and his own philosophical agenda. Nevertheless, the trial of Socrates remains a seminal event in the history of philosophy and law. It is a testament to the enduring power of ideas and the complexities of human society, where the pursuit of truth can sometimes come into conflict with the prevailing norms and values. Socrates' legacy, preserved through the writings of his followers, continues to influence philosophical thought and the principles of justice, making his trial a timeless subject of study and reflection.

Chapter 2: The Salem Witch Trials

The Salem Witch Trials were a series of hearings and prosecutions of people accused of witchcraft in colonial Massachusetts between February 1692 and May 1693. The trials are among the most infamous cases of mass hysteria and injustice in American history. The backdrop for these events was the town of Salem Village, now present-day Danvers, Massachusetts. The community was characterized by a rigid Puritan faith, a theocratic government, and a deep fear of the devil and witchcraft, which were believed to be real and present dangers. This religious and social context created a fertile ground for suspicion and paranoia.

The spark that ignited the Salem Witch Trials came in January 1692, when a group of young girls in Salem Village, including Elizabeth Parris and Abigail Williams, the daughter and niece of Reverend Samuel Parris, began exhibiting strange behaviors. They experienced fits, screamed, threw things, and made strange sounds, symptoms that the local doctor, William Griggs, attributed to supernatural causes, declaring them to be bewitched. The girls, likely influenced by societal expectations and the tense, superstitious atmosphere, accused several women of witchcraft, claiming these women were tormenting them.

The first three women accused were Tituba, an enslaved woman from Barbados who worked for the Parris family; Sarah Good, a homeless beggar; and Sarah Osborne, an elderly, infirm woman who had previously been involved in legal disputes with the Putnam family, one of the most influential families in Salem Village. These initial accusations set a dangerous precedent, as the accused were marginal figures in the community, making it easier for society to believe the accusations against them. The trials quickly escalated, as fear and suspicion spread throughout the community. The court system at the time was ill-equipped to handle such cases, lacking a formal legal framework for dealing with accusations of witchcraft. The court relied heavily on spectral evidence, a controversial and dubious form of evidence based on the testimony of accusers who claimed they saw the specter or spirit of the accused committing witchcraft. This type of evidence was highly subjective and prone to manipulation.

In an environment charged with fear and superstition, accusations began to spiral. The afflicted girls and other accusers expanded their claims, implicating more and more people. The accused ranged from poor, marginalized women to prominent members of the community, including Martha Corey and Rebecca Nurse, both of whom were respected church members. Even Giles Corey, Martha's husband, was accused, and he famously refused to plead, resulting in his brutal death by pressing, where heavy stones were placed on his chest until he died. The role of the courts and the authorities in Salem and the wider Massachusetts Bay Colony was pivotal. The initial hearings were overseen by local magistrates, but as the number of accusations grew, a special Court of Oyer and Terminer was established in June 1692 to handle the cases. This court, presided over by figures such as Judge Samuel Sewall and Judge Samuel Phips, was known for its harsh procedures and willingness to accept spectral evidence. The trials were marked by intense and often chaotic courtroom scenes, with dramatic accusations, fainting fits, and public confessions.

The consequences of the trials were severe and far-reaching. By the end of the trials, 19 people had been hanged, one person had been pressed to death, and several others had died in jail awaiting trial or execution. The community was deeply scarred, and the families of the accused and executed faced social ostracism, loss of property, and lasting stigma. The aftermath of the trials led to a period of reflection and regret. Many involved, including Judge Samuel Sewall, publicly repented for their roles in the events. In January 1697, the Massachusetts General Court declared a day of fasting and soul-searching for the tragedy. In 1702, the court declared the trials unlawful, and in 1711, the colony passed a bill restoring the rights and good names of those accused and granting financial restitution to their heirs. However, the damage done to the community and to the reputations of the accused could never be fully undone.

Several factors contributed to the intensity and spread of the Salem witch hysteria. The Puritan belief system, which emphasized the reality of the devil and the sinful nature of humanity, played a crucial role. The Puritans believed that they were engaged in a constant battle against evil forces, and any deviation from religious orthodoxy could be seen as a sign of witchcraft. This belief system was compounded by the political and social turmoil of the time. The colony was in a state of flux, with political instability, frontier wars with Native American tribes, and a recent smallpox epidemic creating a climate of fear and uncertainty. The socio-economic tensions between Salem Village and the more prosperous Salem Town also fueled the crisis. The village was largely agricultural and conservative, while the town was more mercantile and liberal. The witchcraft accusations often reflected these divisions, with many of the accusers coming from Salem Village and the accused from Salem Town. This socio-economic divide contributed to the suspicion and resentment that fueled the accusations.

Another important aspect of the Salem Witch Trials was the role of gender. The majority of the accused were women, reflecting the gender biases of the time. Women who did not conform to the social norms of Puritan society, such as being outspoken, independent, or involved in disputes, were more likely to be accused. The trials highlighted the precarious position of women in Puritan society, where they could easily become scapegoats for larger social anxieties. The Salem Witch Trials have become a symbol of the dangers of isolationism, religious extremism, and the breakdown of due process under conditions of fear and hysteria. They serve as a cautionary tale about the consequences of allowing superstition and irrationality to override reason and justice. The trials have been the subject of extensive historical analysis and have inspired numerous works of literature, including Arthur Miller's play "The Crucible," which used the trials as an allegory for the McCarthy-era witch hunts in the United States.

Chapter 3: The Trial of Galileo Galilei

The Trial of Galileo Galilei is one of the most renowned episodes in the history of science and the relationship between science and religion. Galileo, an Italian astronomer, physicist, and polymath, became a central figure in the conflict between the Copernican heliocentric model of the universe and the traditional geocentric model endorsed by the Catholic Church. This trial, which occurred in 1633, is emblematic of the tensions between emerging scientific knowledge and established religious doctrines.

Galileo's journey toward trial began with his support for the heliocentric theory proposed by Nicolaus Copernicus in the early 16th century. Copernicus had posited that the Earth and other planets revolve around the Sun, challenging the long-held geocentric model that placed Earth at the center of the universe, a view largely supported by the Catholic Church. Galileo's own observations with the telescope, an instrument he significantly improved, provided strong evidence for the Copernican system. His discoveries included the phases of Venus, the moons of Jupiter, and the rough surface of the Moon, all of which contradicted the geocentric model and the Aristotelian physics that underpinned it.

In 1610, Galileo published his findings in the "Sidereus Nuncius" (The Starry Messenger), which brought him considerable fame but also scrutiny from the Church. The Catholic Church, at the time, was engaged in the Counter-Reformation, a movement to reaffirm its doctrines in response to the Protestant Reformation. This period was marked by an increasing emphasis on doctrinal conformity, and the Church viewed the Copernican theory as not only scientifically controversial but also theologically problematic. The heliocentric model seemed to contradict the literal interpretation of certain scriptures, such as the passages in the Bible that describe the Sun standing still, as in the Book of Joshua.

The first significant confrontation came in 1616, when Galileo was admonished by the Church. Cardinal Robert Bellarmine, a leading theologian, delivered a formal admonition to Galileo, instructing him to abandon the Copernican theory and to refrain from teaching, discussing, or writing about it. The Church also declared the Copernican model "formally heretical" because it seemed to contradict Holy Scripture. Galileo complied with the order publicly, though privately he continued to believe in and study the Copernican system.

The situation escalated in the early 1630s when Galileo published "Dialogue Concerning the Two Chief World Systems," a work that defended the Copernican theory and critiqued the Aristotelian geocentric model. The book was structured as a dialogue among three characters: Salviati, who argues for the Copernican system; Sagredo, an open-minded layman; and Simplicio, a supporter of the geocentric view. The name "Simplicio" (suggesting "simpleton") and the character's portrayal were seen by many as a direct mockery of Pope Urban VIII, who had supported Galileo earlier in his career but had become more conservative under the pressures of the Counter-Reformation.

The publication of the "Dialogue" brought Galileo to the attention of the Roman Inquisition. In 1633, he was summoned to Rome to stand trial for suspicion of heresy. The trial was not only a judicial proceeding but also a significant cultural event, reflecting the broader conflict between the new science and traditional religious beliefs. The main charge against Galileo was his violation of the 1616 edict that prohibited him from teaching or advocating the Copernican theory. The Inquisition accused him of defending the theory in the "Dialogue" and of teaching it as truth, rather than as a mere hypothesis.

Galileo defended himself by arguing that the "Dialogue" presented the Copernican system as a theoretical model rather than an established fact. He also claimed that he had not intended to defy the Church's 1616 injunction, suggesting that any apparent defense of Copernicanism in his book was purely hypothetical. However, the

Inquisition had evidence, including a signed deposition, indicating that Galileo had indeed been prohibited from teaching Copernicanism in any form. The trial was swift, and Galileo was found guilty of "vehement suspicion of heresy." On June 22, 1633, Galileo was forced to recant his views publicly. According to popular legend, after his recantation, Galileo muttered the famous phrase, "E pur si muove" ("And yet it moves"), though this story is likely apocryphal. Galileo was sentenced to house arrest for the remainder of his life, a punishment he served in his villa in Arcetri, near Florence. His works were banned, and the "Dialogue" was placed on the Index of Forbidden Books.

Despite his recantation, Galileo continued his scientific work while under house arrest. He wrote "Two New Sciences," which laid the groundwork for classical mechanics and was smuggled out and published in the Netherlands. This work further established Galileo's reputation as a pioneering scientist, though it did not directly address the Copernican theory. The impact of Galileo's trial was profound and long-lasting. It marked a significant moment in the history of the relationship between science and religion, symbolizing the conflict between free inquiry and doctrinal authority. The trial demonstrated the Church's resistance to new scientific ideas that challenged its teachings, and it underscored the precarious position of scientists who sought to explore and explain the natural world in ways that contradicted established religious doctrines.

In the centuries following Galileo's trial, his case became emblematic of the struggle for intellectual freedom and the separation of science and religion. The Church's condemnation of Galileo was seen by many as a cautionary tale about the dangers of religious interference in scientific inquiry. It was not until 1822 that the Catholic Church officially lifted the ban on books advocating the Copernican system, and in 1992, Pope John Paul II formally acknowledged the Church's errors in the Galileo affair, expressing regret for how the situation was handled.

The trial of Galileo Galilei remains a pivotal event in the history of science, symbolizing the complex and often contentious relationship between scientific innovation and religious belief. Galileo's work laid the foundations for modern physics and astronomy, and his trial highlighted the importance of protecting intellectual freedom and promoting open inquiry. His legacy endures not only in the realm of science but also in the broader cultural and philosophical discussions about the nature of truth, authority, and the pursuit of knowledge. The trial serves as a reminder of the challenges that arise when new ideas challenge established paradigms and the importance of maintaining a dialogue between different ways of understanding the world.

Chapter 4: The Dreyfus Affair

The Dreyfus Affair was a major political scandal that erupted in France in the late 19th and early 20th centuries. It centered around the wrongful conviction of Captain Alfred Dreyfus, a Jewish officer in the French Army, for treason. The affair became a flashpoint for deep-seated tensions in French society, including issues of anti-Semitism, military justice, and the role of the press and public opinion in politics. The Dreyfus Affair had far-reaching implications for French politics and society, and its repercussions were felt well into the 20th century.

The Dreyfus Affair began in 1894 when French military intelligence discovered evidence that military secrets were being passed to the German Embassy in Paris. This evidence came in the form of a torn-up letter, known as the "bordereau," which was found in a wastebasket at the German Embassy. The contents of the bordereau suggested that a French officer was providing confidential information to the Germans. The French Army's General Staff, seeking a quick resolution, focused their suspicions on Captain Alfred Dreyfus, a promising young artillery officer. Dreyfus was chosen as the prime suspect largely due to his Jewish background, which made him an outsider in a predominantly Catholic and often anti-Semitic military establishment. Dreyfus was arrested and subjected to a secret court-martial. The evidence against him was circumstantial and included a handwriting analysis that was later proven to be flawed. Despite the lack of concrete evidence, Dreyfus was convicted of treason on December 22, 1894. He was sentenced to life imprisonment and exiled to Devil's Island, a notorious penal colony off the coast of French Guiana.

The case might have ended there, but doubts about Dreyfus's guilt soon began to surface. In 1896, new evidence emerged that pointed to another officer, Major Ferdinand Walsin Esterhazy, as the real culprit behind the leaking of military secrets. The French military, however, was more concerned with protecting its reputation than admitting to a mistake. The General Staff suppressed the new evidence and actively worked to cover up Esterhazy's guilt. When Esterhazy was eventually brought to trial in 1898, he was acquitted in a rapid and blatantly biased court-martial. The Dreyfus Affair might have remained a relatively obscure miscarriage of justice had it not been for the actions of a group of individuals who were determined to see justice done. Among them was Lieutenant Colonel Georges Picquart, the head of military intelligence who had discovered the evidence implicating Esterhazy. Picquart became convinced of Dreyfus's innocence and tried to expose the truth, but he was silenced by his superiors and transferred to a remote posting.

The most famous of Dreyfus's defenders was the writer Émile Zola, who published an open letter titled "J'accuse...!" on January 13, 1898. Addressed to the President of France, the letter accused the military and the government of a massive cover-up and detailed the injustices committed against Dreyfus. Zola's letter was a turning point in the Dreyfus Affair, as it brought the case to the forefront of public consciousness and polarized French society. The publication of "J'accuse...!" led to Zola being prosecuted for libel, for which he was convicted and fled to England to avoid imprisonment. The Dreyfus Affair divided French society into two camps: the Dreyfusards, who believed in Dreyfus's innocence and sought justice, and the anti-Dreyfusards, who believed that Dreyfus was guilty and that the honor of the army should be protected at all costs. The affair became a battleground for broader issues, including the role of the military in society, the influence of the Catholic Church, and the question of French national identity. It also exposed the virulent anti-Semitism that was prevalent in French society at the time, with many anti-Dreyfusards using the affair to express their distrust and hatred of Jews.

The Dreyfus Affair was marked by a series of legal battles, public demonstrations, and political machinations. Dreyfus's supporters, including his family and a growing number of intellectuals and journalists, continued to press for a retrial. In 1899, Dreyfus was brought back to France for a second court-martial. Despite the overwhelming evidence of his innocence, he was again found guilty, though with "extenuating circumstances," and sentenced to ten years' imprisonment. However, public opinion had shifted significantly, and under pressure, the French President granted Dreyfus a pardon. Dreyfus accepted the pardon but continued to fight to clear his name completely. The affair did not officially conclude until 1906, when the French Supreme Court annulled Dreyfus's conviction and fully exonerated him. He was reinstated in the army with the rank of major and was awarded the Legion of Honour. Despite his reinstatement, Dreyfus's career and life had been irrevocably damaged by the ordeal, and the divisions within French society persisted long after his exoneration.

The Dreyfus Affair had significant and lasting impacts on French politics and society. It exposed the deep-seated anti-Semitism within the French military and broader society, leading to a reassessment of the role of Jews in French public life. The affair also had a profound impact on the French left, which became more secular and more committed to the defense of individual rights and the rule of law. The Dreyfusards, who included many prominent intellectuals, writers, and politicians, became the foundation of what would later be known as the French Radical Party, a key force in early 20th-century French politics. The affair also had international repercussions, influencing public opinion and political movements outside of France. The Dreyfus Affair highlighted the dangers of nationalism, militarism, and xenophobia, serving as a warning to other nations about the potential consequences of such ideologies. It also inspired Jewish leaders and intellectuals, such as Theodor Herzl, to advocate for Zionism and the establishment of a Jewish homeland, as they saw the affair as evidence that Jews could never fully assimilate or be accepted in European societies.

In addition, the Dreyfus Affair had a significant impact on the development of the French legal and judicial systems. The scandal led to reforms aimed at ensuring greater transparency and fairness in legal proceedings, particularly in military courts. The role of the press and public opinion in influencing legal and political outcomes was also recognized and debated, with the affair serving as an early example of the power of media in shaping public discourse. The Dreyfus Affair remains a powerful symbol of the struggle for justice and human rights, and it continues to be a subject of historical and cultural significance. It serves as a reminder of the dangers of prejudice and the importance of standing up against injustice, even when it is supported by powerful institutions and widespread public opinion. The affair also highlights the complexities of national identity and the challenges of balancing loyalty to one's country with the principles of justice and truth.

Chapter 5: The Scopes Monkey Trial

The Scopes Monkey Trial, officially known as The State of Tennessee v. John Thomas Scopes, was a landmark legal case in 1925 that tested the constitutionality of the Butler Act, a Tennessee law that prohibited the teaching of evolution in public schools. The trial is famously associated with the broader conflict between modernist and traditionalist perspectives in American society, particularly regarding science and religion. The case became a major public spectacle and is often seen as a pivotal moment in the American cultural and educational landscape.

The origins of the Scopes Monkey Trial lie in the social and intellectual movements of the early 20th century. The United States was experiencing rapid urbanization and modernization, which brought about significant changes in attitudes and beliefs. This period saw the rise of the scientific community and the spread of Darwin's theory of evolution, which challenged traditional religious views about the creation of life. At the same time, there was a strong fundamentalist Christian movement that sought to reaffirm traditional beliefs and resist the encroachment of modern scientific ideas. This movement was particularly strong in the American South and Midwest, where traditional religious values were deeply rooted.

The Butler Act, passed in Tennessee in March 1925, was a reflection of these tensions. Named after its sponsor, John Washington Butler, the law made it illegal to teach "any theory that denies the story of the Divine Creation of man as taught in the Bible, and to teach instead that man has descended from a lower order of animals." The Act was specifically aimed at preventing the teaching of Charles Darwin's theory of evolution, which was increasingly being included in biology curricula. The American Civil Liberties Union (ACLU) viewed the Butler Act as a violation of academic freedom and an infringement on the separation of church and state. Seeking to challenge the law, the ACLU offered to defend any teacher willing to violate it. John

T. Scopes, a young high school science teacher in Dayton, Tennessee, volunteered to be the test case. Scopes was persuaded by local businessmen who saw the trial as an opportunity to bring publicity and economic benefits to their town.

The trial began on July 10, 1925, and quickly gained national attention. The defense team was led by Clarence Darrow, one of the most famous defense attorneys in the United States, known for his agnostic views and commitment to civil liberties. Darrow was determined to challenge the constitutionality of the Butler Act and to use the trial as a platform to advocate for the teaching of evolution and intellectual freedom. On the prosecution side was William Jennings Bryan, a three-time Democratic presidential candidate, former Secretary of State, and a leading figure in the fundamentalist movement. Bryan was a devout Christian and a staunch opponent of Darwinism, which he believed undermined religious faith and moral values. He had been instrumental in promoting anti-evolution laws like the Butler Act across the country.

The Scopes Trial quickly became a media circus, attracting journalists, intellectuals, and curious onlookers from across the country. The small town of Dayton was inundated with visitors, and the trial was covered extensively by the press, with daily updates and editorials appearing in newspapers nationwide. The courtroom was packed with spectators, and the proceedings were even broadcast live on the radio, a first for any trial in the United States. The trial's most famous moment came when Clarence Darrow called William Jennings Bryan to the stand as an expert witness on the Bible. This move was highly unorthodox, as it was unusual for a prosecutor to testify in the same trial. The exchange between Darrow and Bryan was dramatic and intense, highlighting the stark differences between the scientific and religious worldviews. Darrow questioned Bryan on the literal interpretation of the Bible, challenging him to reconcile biblical accounts with scientific evidence. Bryan's answers revealed the challenges of defending a literal interpretation of the Bible in the face of modern scientific understanding. For instance, when Darrow asked Bryan about the age of the Earth, Bryan conceded that the "days" mentioned in the Genesis creation story might not be literal 24-hour days but could represent longer periods of time.

Despite the drama of the trial and the intense public interest, the legal outcome was relatively straightforward. The jury found John Scopes guilty of violating the Butler Act, and he was fined $100, the minimum penalty under the law. The verdict was widely expected, as Scopes had openly admitted to teaching evolution, and the law itself was clear. However, the trial was far from a simple legal proceeding; it was a public debate on the broader issues of science, religion, and education. The trial's immediate legal impact was limited. In 1927, the Tennessee Supreme Court overturned Scopes's conviction on a technicality, ruling that the judge, rather than the jury, had improperly imposed the fine. The court, however, upheld the constitutionality of the Butler Act, and the law remained in effect in Tennessee until 1967. Despite this, the trial had a lasting cultural and social impact. It highlighted the growing divide between scientific and religious communities in the United States and brought the debate over evolution and creationism into the national spotlight. The trial also underscored the tension between rural and urban values, with the media often portraying the town of Dayton and its residents in a stereotypically negative light, reinforcing existing prejudices about the rural South.

The Scopes Monkey Trial had a profound influence on public opinion and the discourse surrounding science and religion. While the trial did not immediately change educational policies or laws, it marked the beginning of a shift in the public's perception of the relationship between science and religion. Over time, the teaching of evolution became more accepted in American public schools, though controversies and debates continued, particularly in certain regions and among particular groups. The trial also had a significant impact on the careers and legacies of those involved. Clarence Darrow became even more famous for his role in the trial, solidifying his reputation as a defender of civil liberties and intellectual freedom. William Jennings Bryan, on the other hand, faced criticism for his performance, particularly for his inability to effectively argue against Darrow's questioning on the stand. Bryan died just five days after the trial ended, and while he remained a respected figure among many fundamentalists, the trial marked a decline in his influence on the national stage.

The Scopes Monkey Trial has continued to be a reference point in discussions about the teaching of evolution, the role of religion in public life, and the limits of academic freedom. The trial has been the subject of numerous books, articles, and plays, most notably the play and film "Inherit the Wind," which dramatizes the events of the trial and explores its themes. The trial is often cited in debates over the separation of church and state, serving as a reminder of the potential conflicts that can arise when religious and scientific perspectives clash. In the decades following the trial, the debate over the teaching of evolution in public schools continued to evolve. In the 1960s and 1970s, the United States Supreme Court ruled in several cases that prohibitions on the teaching of evolution and the mandatory inclusion of creationism in public school curricula violated the Establishment Clause of the First Amendment, which prohibits the government from endorsing any particular religion. These rulings effectively invalidated laws like the Butler Act and helped establish the principle that public education should be based on scientific evidence rather than religious doctrine.

The Scopes Monkey Trial is a landmark in American legal and cultural history, representing a critical moment in the ongoing struggle between scientific understanding and religious belief, and the broader question of how to reconcile these two ways of knowing. It serves as a reminder of the importance of intellectual freedom, the complexities of cultural change, and the challenges of balancing respect for religious beliefs with the need to teach scientifically accurate information in public education. The trial's legacy continues to influence debates about science, education, and religion in the United States and beyond, making it a case study in the intersections of law, culture, and ideology.

Chapter 6: Brown v Board of Education

Brown v. Board of Education is one of the most significant and landmark Supreme Court cases in United States history. Decided on May 17, 1954, this case was pivotal in the struggle for civil rights and the desegregation of American public schools. It overturned the "separate but equal" doctrine established by the Plessy v. Ferguson decision in 1896, fundamentally changing the landscape of American public education and society as a whole.

The roots of the case trace back to the systemic racial segregation prevalent in the United States, particularly in the Southern states, following the Civil War and Reconstruction. After the Reconstruction era ended, Jim Crow laws were enacted across the South, legally enforcing racial segregation in public facilities, including schools. The Plessy v. Ferguson decision by the Supreme Court had declared that segregation was constitutional as long as the facilities provided to each race were "equal." This doctrine, however, was deeply flawed in practice, as the facilities and resources allocated to African American students were consistently inferior compared to those provided to white students.

By the mid-20th century, the NAACP (National Association for the Advancement of Colored People) had become a prominent organization advocating for civil rights and challenging racial segregation through the legal system. Under the leadership of attorneys such as Thurgood Marshall, who would later become the first African American Supreme Court Justice, the NAACP began to strategically challenge the "separate but equal" doctrine, particularly in the realm of public education. The NAACP sought to demonstrate that segregated schools were inherently unequal and violated the Equal Protection Clause of the 14th Amendment, which guarantees all citizens "equal protection of the laws."

The Brown v. Board of Education case was actually a consolidation of five different cases from different states, all challenging the constitutionality of racial segregation in public schools. The cases came from Delaware, Kansas, South Carolina, Virginia, and Washington D.C. The lead case involved Oliver Brown, an African American parent from Topeka, Kansas, who filed a lawsuit after his daughter, Linda Brown, was denied entry to an all-white elementary school close to their home. Instead, Linda was forced to attend a segregated black school further away, which lacked the resources and facilities available at the white school.

The NAACP's legal team argued that segregated schools were inherently unequal and that segregation itself had detrimental effects on African American children, instilling a sense of inferiority and hindering their educational and personal development. They presented evidence from various studies, including the famous doll experiments conducted by psychologists Kenneth and Mamie Clark. In these experiments, black children were given the choice between white and black dolls and consistently showed a preference for white dolls, indicating internalized racism and feelings of inferiority caused by segregation.

The case reached the Supreme Court, where it was heard over several sessions. On May 17, 1954, the Supreme Court, led by Chief Justice Earl Warren, delivered a unanimous 9-0 decision stating that racial segregation in public schools violated the Equal Protection Clause of the 14th Amendment. The Court declared that "separate educational facilities are inherently unequal" and that segregation was harmful to African American children, depriving them of equal educational opportunities. The Court's decision in Brown v. Board of Education did not immediately desegregate American public schools. Instead, it marked the beginning of a long and difficult process of dismantling institutionalized racial segregation in education and other public domains. The ruling met with strong resistance in many

Southern states, where segregation was deeply entrenched in the social and political fabric. Many states employed a variety of tactics to delay or avoid desegregation, including the implementation of "massive resistance" strategies, which involved the closure of public schools and the creation of private, whites-only academies.

To address the widespread resistance and slow pace of desegregation, the Supreme Court issued a second ruling in 1955, known as Brown II. In this decision, the Court ordered that desegregation occur "with all deliberate speed," but this vague wording allowed for significant delays and continued resistance. In the years following the Brown decision, the federal government, civil rights activists, and African American communities faced numerous challenges in enforcing the ruling. The Civil Rights Movement gained momentum, with organizations like the NAACP, the Southern Christian Leadership Conference (SCLC), and the Student Nonviolent Coordinating Committee (SNCC) leading efforts to end segregation and secure equal rights for African Americans. Key events, such as the Montgomery Bus Boycott, the Freedom Rides, and the March on Washington, highlighted the growing demand for civil rights and equality.

The Brown decision also had a profound impact on the legal and cultural landscape of the United States. It laid the groundwork for subsequent civil rights legislation, including the Civil Rights Act of 1964 and the Voting Rights Act of 1965, which sought to eliminate racial discrimination and protect the rights of African Americans. The case also set a legal precedent for challenging other forms of discrimination, including those based on gender, disability, and sexual orientation.

However, the legacy of Brown v. Board of Education is complex and reflects the ongoing struggle for racial equality in America. While the case was a crucial victory for civil rights, it also exposed the limitations of legal action in addressing deeply ingrained social and economic inequalities. Many schools and communities continued to practice de facto segregation, even if de jure (legal) segregation was officially abolished. The phenomenon of "white flight"—the migration of white families from urban areas to suburban regions—exacerbated racial segregation in schools, as public schools in many urban areas became predominantly African American and underfunded, while suburban schools remained predominantly white and well-resourced.

In the decades following the Brown decision, various court cases and policies attempted to address these disparities. The implementation of busing programs aimed to integrate schools by transporting students from different neighborhoods, but these efforts often met with controversy and opposition. In some cases, the Supreme Court limited the scope of desegregation efforts, such as in the 1974 case Milliken v. Bradley, which ruled that desegregation plans could not mandate busing across district lines unless it was proven that multiple districts had implemented policies explicitly designed to enforce segregation.

Today, the issues raised by Brown v. Board of Education remain relevant, as debates over educational equity, racial disparities, and the role of race in American society continue. The case is frequently cited in discussions about affirmative action, the achievement gap between white and minority students, and the ongoing challenges of ensuring equal access to quality education for all children. Despite significant progress since the Brown decision, disparities in educational opportunities and outcomes persist, often reflecting broader systemic issues such as economic inequality, residential segregation, and unequal funding for public schools.

Brown v. Board of Education is a landmark case not only for its legal significance but also for its role in shaping the national consciousness around issues of race and justice. It serves as a reminder of both the power and the limitations of the legal system in addressing social injustices. The case also underscores the importance of grassroots activism, public engagement, and political will in driving social change. The story of Brown is not just a historical episode; it is an ongoing narrative that challenges each generation to confront and address the inequalities that persist in American society.

In reflecting on the Brown decision, it is crucial to recognize the courage and resilience of the individuals and communities who fought for justice and equality, often at great personal risk. The case stands as a testament to the enduring struggle for civil rights and serves as an inspiration for continued efforts to create a more just and equitable society. As we look to the future, the lessons of Brown v. Board of Education remind us of the importance of vigilance, advocacy, and the collective pursuit of justice in the face of adversity.

Chapter 7: Roe v Wade

Roe v. Wade, decided by the United States Supreme Court on January 22, 1973, is one of the most consequential and controversial legal decisions in American history. This landmark ruling recognized a woman's constitutional right to privacy in making medical decisions, including the choice to have an abortion. The case not only transformed American law but also ignited a national debate over reproductive rights, privacy, morality, and the role of the state in personal medical decisions. The decision continues to resonate in the political, legal, and social spheres of the United States and beyond.

The roots of the Roe v. Wade case can be traced back to the broader context of the women's rights movement of the 1960s and 1970s. During this period, the movement was gaining momentum, advocating for greater gender equality, including issues related to reproductive health and rights. Before Roe, abortion laws in the United States varied widely from state to state. Many states had strict laws prohibiting or severely restricting abortion, with exceptions typically only in cases where the mother's life was in danger. These restrictive laws forced many women to seek unsafe and illegal abortions, leading to significant health risks and, in some cases, death. The situation highlighted a pressing need for legal reform to protect women's health and autonomy.

The case of Roe v. Wade began when "Jane Roe," a pseudonym for Norma McCorvey, a Texas woman seeking an abortion, challenged the state's restrictive abortion laws. At the time, Texas law permitted abortion only when it was necessary to save the mother's life. McCorvey, who was pregnant and did not want to carry the pregnancy to term, could not afford to travel to another state where abortion might be legal under less restrictive circumstances. Unable to secure a safe and legal abortion in Texas, McCorvey's situation became the basis for challenging the constitutionality of the state's abortion laws.

She filed a lawsuit against Henry Wade, the Dallas County District Attorney, who was responsible for enforcing the state's criminal abortion laws.

The case quickly gained the attention of feminist activists and legal advocates. It was taken up by attorneys Linda Coffee and Sarah Weddington, who sought to argue that Texas's abortion laws were unconstitutional. They contended that the laws violated a woman's right to privacy, as protected by the Due Process Clause of the Fourteenth Amendment, and that this right extended to a woman's decision to terminate her pregnancy. The case made its way through the legal system and eventually reached the United States Supreme Court.

On January 22, 1973, the Supreme Court issued a 7-2 decision in favor of "Jane Roe." The opinion, written by Justice Harry Blackmun, was a complex and carefully crafted document that sought to balance the rights of women with the state's interests. The Court held that the right to privacy, which it had recognized in earlier cases involving marriage, contraception, and child-rearing, extended to a woman's decision to have an abortion. However, the Court also acknowledged that this right was not absolute and must be balanced against the state's interests in protecting women's health and prenatal life.

To navigate this balance, the Supreme Court established a trimester framework for regulating abortion. In the first trimester of pregnancy, the Court ruled that the decision to have an abortion should be left entirely to the woman and her physician. During the second trimester, the state could regulate abortion procedures in ways that were reasonably related to maternal health. In the third trimester, once the fetus reached the point of "viability" (the ability to survive outside the womb), the state's interest in protecting potential life became compelling, and it could regulate or even prohibit abortions, except when necessary to protect the life or health of the mother.

The Roe v. Wade decision was a watershed moment in American jurisprudence, dramatically altering the legal landscape regarding reproductive rights. It effectively invalidated many existing state laws that restricted abortion and established a woman's right to choose as a fundamental constitutional right. The decision sparked immediate and intense reactions from both supporters and opponents of abortion rights. Proponents of the decision, including many women's rights activists and civil liberties advocates, hailed it as a major victory for women's autonomy and privacy. They argued that the decision was a crucial step towards ensuring that women could make personal medical decisions without government interference.

Opponents of the decision, however, viewed it as a moral and legal overreach. Many religious and pro-life groups argued that the ruling undermined the sanctity of life and the state's interest in protecting unborn children. They contended that the decision effectively created a constitutional right to abortion, which they believed was neither intended nor supported by the Constitution's framers. The decision galvanized the pro-life movement, which sought to overturn or limit the scope of Roe through legal challenges, legislative action, and public advocacy.

In the years following Roe v. Wade, the abortion debate became a central issue in American politics, deeply dividing the country along ideological, religious, and cultural lines. The decision also led to a series of subsequent legal battles and Supreme Court cases that further refined and, in some cases, limited the scope of the right to abortion. For instance, in Planned Parenthood v. Casey (1992), the Supreme Court reaffirmed the core holding of Roe that women have a right to choose an abortion before fetal viability. However, the Court also replaced the trimester framework with an "undue burden" standard, allowing states to impose regulations on abortion as long as they did not place an undue burden on a woman's ability to obtain an abortion. This decision allowed for greater state regulation of abortion, leading to a proliferation of state laws imposing various restrictions, such as waiting periods, parental consent requirements, and mandatory counseling.

The legal, social, and political landscape surrounding abortion rights continued to evolve in the decades after Roe and Casey. The appointment of more conservative judges to the Supreme Court and lower federal courts led to concerns among abortion rights advocates about the potential erosion or outright overturning of Roe v. Wade. Meanwhile, opponents of abortion rights continued to push for state and federal laws that would restrict or ban abortion, often framing their arguments around protecting the health of women and the rights of the unborn.

The Roe decision also had significant implications beyond the United States. It influenced legal and policy debates about reproductive rights in other countries and became a reference point in discussions about women's rights and health globally. The decision underscored the interconnectedness of legal, medical, and ethical considerations in the regulation of reproductive health and highlighted the challenges of balancing individual rights with societal interests.

Despite its centrality in American legal and cultural discourse, Roe v. Wade has always been a contentious and polarizing issue. The decision's impact extends beyond the legal realm, influencing politics, public policy, and social movements. It has shaped the agendas of political parties, influenced judicial appointments, and mobilized advocacy groups on both sides of the abortion debate. The case also highlights the broader question of judicial interpretation and the role of the Supreme Court in addressing contentious social issues. Critics of Roe argue that the Court overstepped its bounds by effectively creating a new constitutional right, while supporters contend that the decision was a necessary protection of individual liberties against state interference.

As of the early 21st century, Roe v. Wade remains a focal point of ongoing legal and political battles. The rise of more conservative judicial appointments, particularly to the Supreme Court, has led to heightened scrutiny of Roe and concerns about its potential reversal. The passing of state laws aimed at challenging the boundaries set by Roe and Casey has prompted new legal challenges, setting the stage for potential Supreme Court rulings that could further define or restrict abortion rights in the United States.

The legacy of Roe v. Wade is multifaceted. It is a landmark in the struggle for women's rights and reproductive autonomy, a flashpoint in the ongoing cultural wars over moral and ethical values, and a significant chapter in the history of constitutional law. The decision's impact on American society, law, and politics continues to be profound, reflecting the deep and enduring complexities of issues related to reproductive rights, personal autonomy, and the role of government in regulating intimate aspects of individuals' lives.

Chapter 8: The Nuremberg Trials

The Nuremberg Trials were a series of military tribunals held after World War II to bring Nazi war criminals to justice. These trials, conducted in the city of Nuremberg, Germany, from 1945 to 1946, were unprecedented in history, as they represented the first time that an international court prosecuted individuals for crimes against humanity, war crimes, and genocide. The trials were a crucial step in establishing principles of international law and accountability for leaders and officials who commit atrocities. They also laid the foundation for subsequent human rights jurisprudence and the development of international criminal law.

The origins of the Nuremberg Trials can be traced back to the atrocities committed during World War II, particularly the Holocaust, where millions of Jews, along with other minorities and political dissidents, were systematically exterminated by the Nazi regime. As the Allied forces began to liberate concentration camps and uncover evidence of mass atrocities, the world was shocked by the scale and brutality of the Nazi crimes. The Allied powers—comprising the United States, the Soviet Union, the United Kingdom, and France—recognized the need to hold those responsible for these crimes accountable. However, they faced significant challenges in determining how to prosecute the perpetrators. Unlike previous conflicts, the crimes committed during World War II were of such an unprecedented scale and nature that existing legal frameworks were insufficient.

The concept of trying war criminals in an international court was a novel idea. Previous efforts to hold individuals accountable for war crimes, such as after World War I, were limited and largely ineffective. The Allies were determined to establish a legal precedent that would not only punish the perpetrators but also deter future atrocities. After much negotiation, they agreed to establish the International Military Tribunal (IMT) in Nuremberg, Germany. Nuremberg was chosen for its symbolic significance as the site of Nazi rallies and as a city relatively undamaged by the war, with suitable facilities for a large-scale trial.

The legal framework for the Nuremberg Trials was established through the London Charter of the International Military Tribunal, signed on August 8, 1945. The charter defined the crimes to be prosecuted and established the tribunal's jurisdiction and procedures. The crimes were classified into three categories: crimes against peace (planning, initiating, and waging wars of aggression), war crimes (violations of the laws and customs of war, including the treatment of prisoners of war and civilians), and crimes against humanity (including genocide, extermination, enslavement, and other atrocities committed against civilian populations). The charter also outlined the principles of individual accountability, rejecting the defense of superior orders and stating that following orders would not absolve individuals of responsibility if they were involved in criminal activities.

The Nuremberg Trials began on November 20, 1945, with 24 major political and military leaders of Nazi Germany indicted for crimes against peace, war crimes, and crimes against humanity. The most prominent defendants included Hermann Göring, the head of the Luftwaffe and a leading member of the Nazi Party; Rudolf Hess, Hitler's deputy; Joachim von Ribbentrop, the foreign minister; and Wilhelm Keitel, the chief of the High Command of the German Armed Forces. Adolf Hitler, Heinrich Himmler, and Joseph Goebbels, key figures in the Nazi regime, had committed suicide before they could be captured and brought to trial.

The prosecution at Nuremberg was led by Robert H. Jackson, the chief U.S. prosecutor and an Associate Justice of the U.S. Supreme Court. Jackson's opening statement laid out the prosecution's case and the significance of the trial: "That four great nations, flushed with victory and stung with injury, stay the hand of vengeance and voluntarily submit their captives to the judgment of the law is one of the most significant tributes that Power has ever paid to Reason."

The prosecution's case was built on extensive documentary evidence, including captured German records, orders, and reports that detailed the planning and execution of the Nazi war effort and the atrocities committed in the concentration camps.

One of the most significant aspects of the Nuremberg Trials was the introduction of the concept of "crimes against humanity." This category of crimes, which had not been formally recognized in international law before, was critical in addressing the atrocities committed by the Nazis, including the systematic extermination of Jews, Romani people, disabled individuals, and other marginalized groups. The inclusion of crimes against humanity allowed the tribunal to prosecute acts committed both during and before the war that were not directly connected to the war effort but were part of the Nazi regime's genocidal policies.

The defense presented by the accused at Nuremberg varied. Many defendants claimed that they were merely following orders and that they had no choice but to comply with the commands of their superiors. Others argued that the tribunal was a form of "victor's justice," lacking legitimacy because the Allies themselves had committed atrocities during the war, such as the bombing of Dresden or the atomic bombings of Hiroshima and Nagasaki. Some defendants, like Albert Speer, the Minister of Armaments and War Production, expressed remorse and accepted responsibility for their actions, while others, like Göring, remained unrepentant and defiant.

The tribunal faced numerous legal and ethical challenges. One key issue was the principle of **nullum crimen sine lege** ("no crime without law"), which holds that one cannot be prosecuted for an act that was not a crime at the time it was committed. Critics argued that the Nuremberg Trials applied ex post facto laws by prosecuting individuals for crimes like genocide and crimes against humanity, which were not clearly defined in international law before the war. However, the tribunal countered that these crimes were so heinous that they were universally recognized as wrong, even if they had not been formally codified as crimes.

Another challenge was ensuring a fair trial for the defendants. The tribunal aimed to uphold the principles of due process, including the right to counsel, the right to cross-examine witnesses, and the right to present evidence and call witnesses in defense. The trials were conducted with translators and interpreters to ensure that all participants could understand the proceedings, given the international nature of the tribunal and the diversity of languages spoken by the defendants, witnesses, and legal teams.

The verdicts in the Nuremberg Trials were delivered on October 1, 1946. Of the 24 defendants, 12 were sentenced to death, including Göring (who committed suicide the night before his execution), Ribbentrop, and Keitel. Three were acquitted, and the remaining defendants received various prison sentences, ranging from 10 years to life imprisonment. The sentences were carried out swiftly, with the executions taking place on October 16, 1946.

The Nuremberg Trials had a profound impact on international law and the development of mechanisms for prosecuting war crimes and crimes against humanity. They established the precedent that individuals, including heads of state and military leaders, could be held accountable for their actions under international law. The trials also contributed to the creation of key international legal instruments, such as the Genocide Convention (1948) and the Universal Declaration of Human Rights (1948). These documents enshrined principles of human rights and set standards for the treatment of individuals, regardless of nationality, ethnicity, or political affiliation.

The legacy of the Nuremberg Trials extends beyond the immediate post-war period. The principles established at Nuremberg influenced the establishment of subsequent international tribunals, such as the International Criminal Tribunal for the former Yugoslavia (ICTY) and the International Criminal Tribunal for Rwanda (ICTR), which prosecuted individuals responsible for atrocities in those regions during the 1990s. The Nuremberg Trials also laid the groundwork for the establishment of the International Criminal Court (ICC) in 2002, a permanent international court with jurisdiction over crimes of genocide, crimes against humanity, war crimes, and the crime of aggression.

Despite their significance, the Nuremberg Trials were not without controversy and criticism. Some critics argued that the trials were an example of "victor's justice," as only the leaders of the defeated Axis powers were prosecuted, while no Allied leaders were held accountable for actions such as the firebombing of civilian areas or the use of nuclear weapons. Additionally, the Soviet Union, one of the main prosecuting powers, had itself committed numerous atrocities, such as the Katyn massacre and the forced deportation of millions of people, which were not addressed by the tribunal.

Others criticized the selective nature of the trials, noting that many lower-ranking officials and individuals who played significant roles in the Nazi regime's crimes were not prosecuted. The trials were also criticized for their handling of the defense of superior orders, with some arguing that the tribunal's rejection of this defense was overly harsh, given the authoritarian nature of the Nazi state and the severe consequences faced by those who disobeyed orders.

Despite these criticisms, the Nuremberg Trials remain a landmark in the history of international law and justice. They demonstrated the possibility of holding individuals accountable for atrocities, regardless of their rank or position, and underscored the importance of establishing legal standards for the protection of human rights. The trials also served as a stark reminder of the horrors of the Holocaust and the necessity of vigilance in preventing such atrocities from occurring again.

In recent years, the legacy of the Nuremberg Trials has continued to influence discussions on international law, human rights, and transitional justice. The principles established at Nuremberg have been invoked in cases involving crimes against humanity, genocide, and war crimes, and have shaped the development of international criminal jurisprudence. The trials have also inspired efforts to address impunity for crimes committed during conflicts and periods of political repression, emphasizing the importance of accountability and justice for victims.

Chapter 9: The Trial of Joan of Arc

The Trial of Joan of Arc, a landmark event in medieval history, remains a compelling narrative of faith, politics, and the interplay between church and state. Joan of Arc, a young peasant girl from Domrémy in northeastern France, claimed to have received visions from saints instructing her to support Charles VII and help reclaim France from English control during the Hundred Years' War. Her remarkable leadership and victories, especially the lifting of the siege of Orléans in 1429, made her a national heroine and a pivotal figure in the French resistance against English domination.

The trial itself, conducted by the English-backed Bishop Pierre Cauchon, was a complex mixture of ecclesiastical proceedings and political machinations. Held in the city of Rouen, which was under English control, the trial aimed to discredit Joan and undermine the legitimacy of Charles VII, who was crowned king largely due to her influence and military successes. The trial began in January 1431, with Joan facing numerous charges, including heresy, witchcraft, and dressing as a man—an accusation tied to her wearing of military attire.

Joan's trial was heavily biased from the outset, with the tribunal composed largely of pro-English clergy. She was interrogated over several sessions, during which she consistently defended her visions and divine mission. Her responses, noted for their intelligence and coherence, often left her inquisitors confounded. However, the trial was less about discovering the truth and more about producing a desired outcome: Joan's discreditation and execution.

Central to the charges was the allegation of heresy. Joan's claim to divine visions was seen as a direct challenge to the church's authority, and her refusal to submit these visions to ecclesiastical scrutiny was considered obstinate. Furthermore, her wearing of male clothing, even in prison, was construed as a violation of biblical precepts. However,

Joan defended her actions, asserting that her attire was a practical necessity for her safety and that she had acted under divine guidance.

Despite her strong defense, the trial was a foregone conclusion. Joan was eventually forced into signing a confession, which she later recanted, reaffirming her visions and divine mission. This act of recantation was pivotal, as it sealed her fate. On May 30, 1431, Joan was burned at the stake in the marketplace of Rouen, her death intended to serve as a warning to others who might challenge the established order.

The aftermath of Joan's trial was significant. It did not diminish her impact or the role she had played in the French campaign against the English. In fact, her martyrdom only solidified her status as a symbol of French nationalism and resistance. Twenty-five years later, a posthumous retrial ordered by Pope Callixtus III cleared her of all charges, declaring her a martyr who had been wrongfully convicted. This rehabilitation not only restored her reputation but also highlighted the political and judicial manipulation that characterized her original trial.

Joan of Arc's trial is a profound example of how legal and religious institutions can be manipulated to serve political ends. It underscores the dangers faced by individuals who challenge dominant ideologies and the potential for legal systems to be used as tools of oppression. Her story resonates through the centuries as a testament to courage, conviction, and the enduring power of belief. Joan of Arc remains an iconic figure in both religious and secular contexts, symbolizing the struggle for justice and the complexities of human faith and authority. Her trial and execution stand as a stark reminder of the intersections between law, religion, and politics, and the enduring impact these intersections can have on history.

Chapter 10: The OJ Simpson Trial

The O.J. Simpson trial, officially known as the People of the State of California v. Orenthal James Simpson, stands as one of the most publicized and controversial criminal trials in American history. The trial, which took place in 1995, centered on the charges against former professional football player and actor O.J. Simpson for the murders of his ex-wife Nicole Brown Simpson and her friend Ronald Goldman. This case captivated the nation, combining elements of celebrity culture, race relations, and the intricacies of the American legal system.

The incident that led to the trial occurred on June 12, 1994, when Nicole Brown Simpson and Ronald Goldman were found brutally murdered outside Nicole's condominium in the Brentwood area of Los Angeles. The evidence at the scene, including bloody gloves, footprints, and fibers, soon pointed to O.J. Simpson as a prime suspect. Simpson's subsequent actions, such as his infamous low-speed chase in a white Ford Bronco, were broadcast live on national television, dramatically increasing public interest in the case.

The trial began on January 24, 1995, in the Los Angeles County Superior Court, presided over by Judge Lance Ito. The prosecution, led by Marcia Clark and Christopher Darden, presented a compelling case based on physical evidence, including DNA analysis, which linked Simpson to the crime scene. The evidence included blood samples, hair and fiber evidence, and a glove found at Simpson's estate that matched one found at the crime scene. The prosecution argued that Simpson had a history of domestic violence against Nicole, presenting this as a motive for the murders.

However, the defense, led by Robert Shapiro and later dominated by Johnnie Cochran, implemented a highly effective strategy that came to be known as the "Dream Team." The defense argued that Simpson was a victim of police misconduct and racial prejudice, suggesting that evidence was planted or tampered with by the Los Angeles Police

Department (LAPD), specifically targeting LAPD detective Mark Fuhrman, who was accused of being a racist. Fuhrman's use of racial slurs in the past, brought to light during the trial, severely damaged the prosecution's case by casting doubt on the integrity of the police investigation.

The trial was notable not only for its legal drama but also for the intense media coverage and public fascination it generated. The proceedings were televised daily, turning the trial into a national spectacle. Public opinion was sharply divided, often along racial lines, with many African Americans viewing Simpson's trial as a stand against systemic racism in the criminal justice system, while others saw the overwhelming evidence as indicative of his guilt.

A critical moment in the trial was when Simpson was asked to try on the gloves found at the crime scene and his home. The gloves appeared too tight for him, leading to the memorable quote by Cochran during closing arguments: "If it doesn't fit, you must acquit." This demonstration was pivotal in creating reasonable doubt in the minds of the jurors regarding the prosecution's evidence.

After a highly publicized nine-month trial, the jury, consisting of nine African Americans, two whites, and one Hispanic, deliberated for less than four hours before returning a verdict of not guilty on October 3, 1995. The verdict was met with mixed reactions: celebration and relief among Simpson's supporters, particularly in the African American community, and disbelief and outrage among those who believed him guilty.

The O.J. Simpson trial had far-reaching implications beyond the immediate case. It brought to the forefront issues of race, domestic violence, and the influence of media in legal proceedings. The trial exposed deep societal divisions and highlighted disparities in how justice is perceived and administered in the United States. Furthermore, it sparked debates about the effectiveness of the jury system, the ethics of defense strategies, and the role of celebrity in the judicial process.

Years after the trial, Simpson faced a civil lawsuit filed by the families of Nicole Brown Simpson and Ronald Goldman. In 1997, a civil jury found Simpson liable for their wrongful deaths and awarded the families $33.5 million in damages, a decision based on the lower standard of proof required in civil cases compared to criminal trials.

The legacy of the O.J. Simpson trial continues to be felt in American culture and legal studies. It is frequently referenced in discussions about the criminal justice system, media ethics, and racial dynamics in the United States. The case also influenced popular culture, inspiring numerous books, documentaries, and dramatizations, including the acclaimed television series "The People v. O.J. Simpson: American Crime Story."

In later years, Simpson had additional legal troubles, including a 2007 arrest for armed robbery and kidnapping, which led to his conviction and a nine-year prison sentence. This further complicated his public image, blending his earlier celebrity status with his legal controversies. The O.J. Simpson trial remains a critical reference point in understanding the complexities of high-profile criminal cases and their impact on society.

Chapter 11: The Trial of Julius and Ethel Rosenberg

The trial of Julius and Ethel Rosenberg, held in the early 1950s, is one of the most controversial and politically charged espionage cases in American history. The Rosenbergs, a married couple, were accused of passing atomic secrets to the Soviet Union during the Cold War. Their trial, conviction, and eventual execution have sparked decades of debate over issues of justice, espionage, and the influence of anti-communist sentiment in the United States.

The background of the case is rooted in the intense geopolitical rivalry between the United States and the Soviet Union following World War II. The U.S., having emerged from the war with the world's only nuclear arsenal, was keenly aware of the strategic advantage this provided. However, the Soviet Union detonated its first atomic bomb in 1949, far sooner than American intelligence had predicted. This development led to a frenzied search for spies within the U.S. who might have helped the Soviets acquire nuclear secrets.

Julius Rosenberg, an electrical engineer who had worked for the U.S. Army Signal Corps, and his wife, Ethel, were arrested in 1950. Julius was implicated by his brother-in-law, David Greenglass, who admitted to passing classified information to the Soviets and claimed that Julius had recruited him into the spy network. Ethel was accused primarily on the basis of her alleged involvement in typing up the documents that Greenglass provided. The evidence against the Rosenbergs included testimonies from Greenglass and his wife, Ruth, as well as various documents and sketches that purportedly detailed nuclear weapon designs.

The trial began on March 6, 1951, in New York City, presided over by Judge Irving Kaufman. The prosecution, led by Irving Saypol, argued that the Rosenbergs had engaged in a conspiracy to commit espionage by providing the Soviet Union with critical information about the American atomic bomb project, thereby accelerating Soviet nuclear capabilities. The defense, headed by Emanuel Bloch, sought to discredit the testimonies of Greenglass and others, suggesting that they were unreliable witnesses who had altered their stories to gain favor with the government and avoid harsh sentences themselves.

A key aspect of the trial was the context of the Red Scare, a period characterized by widespread fear of communist infiltration in American institutions. This environment contributed to an atmosphere in which the Rosenbergs were viewed not just as potential spies but as existential threats to national security. The prosecution capitalized on this fear, painting the Rosenbergs as traitors who had endangered millions of lives by betraying their country.

The evidence presented at trial was largely circumstantial, particularly against Ethel. Her involvement in the espionage activities, as presented by the prosecution, hinged primarily on the testimony of her brother, David Greenglass, who later admitted to providing false testimony against her under pressure from prosecutors and in an attempt to protect his own wife from prosecution. This aspect of the case has led to ongoing debate about the fairness of the trial and the extent of Ethel's actual involvement in any espionage activities.

Despite these controversies, the jury found both Julius and Ethel Rosenberg guilty of conspiracy to commit espionage on March 29, 1951. Judge Kaufman sentenced them to death, a decision that he justified by stating that their actions had placed "the atomic bomb into the hands of the Russians" and thus had potentially triggered the Korean War. Kaufman suggested that the Rosenbergs' crime was worse than murder because it compromised the security of the United States.

The death sentences sparked international outcry and a significant amount of domestic debate. Many prominent figures and organizations called for clemency, arguing that the evidence, particularly against Ethel, was insufficient to justify the death penalty. Critics of the trial pointed to the influence of the political climate and questioned the motivations behind the prosecution's case. The American Civil Liberties Union and other groups argued that the trial was a miscarriage of justice, reflecting broader anti-communist hysteria rather than a fair legal process.

Despite these appeals, including a petition to President Dwight D. Eisenhower, the sentences were upheld. The Rosenbergs were executed in the electric chair at Sing Sing Correctional Facility on June 19, 1953, becoming the first American civilians to be executed for espionage during peacetime. Their deaths cemented their status as symbols of the Cold War, seen by some as martyrs and by others as traitors.

The legacy of the Rosenberg trial is complex and multifaceted. It has been the subject of numerous books, films, and scholarly analyses, many of which have re-examined the evidence and circumstances surrounding the case. In recent years, declassified Soviet archives and additional testimony have provided more context, suggesting that while Julius Rosenberg was involved in espionage activities, Ethel's role was likely much smaller than portrayed at trial. The case continues to be a touchstone in discussions about civil liberties, due process, and the dangers of political persecution.

The trial of Julius and Ethel Rosenberg remains a powerful illustration of the tensions between national security and individual rights, as well as the impact of political pressures on the judicial process. It is a cautionary tale about the potential for justice to be compromised in times of national fear and uncertainty. The Rosenbergs' story serves as a reminder of the importance of maintaining legal standards and protecting civil liberties, even in the face of perceived existential threats.

Chapter 12: The Trial of Nelson Mandela

The trial of Nelson Mandela, specifically the Rivonia Trial, is one of the most significant events in the history of the anti-apartheid struggle in South Africa. It not only highlighted the oppressive nature of the apartheid regime but also marked a pivotal moment in the international recognition of the fight against racial segregation. Nelson Mandela, along with several other leaders of the African National Congress (ANC), was charged with sabotage, a crime that carried the death penalty. The trial, held from 1963 to 1964, ended with Mandela and his co-defendants being sentenced to life imprisonment, a verdict that transformed them into global symbols of resistance against racial injustice.

The Rivonia Trial is named after Liliesleaf Farm in Rivonia, a suburb of Johannesburg, which served as the secret headquarters of the ANC and its armed wing, Umkhonto we Sizwe (Spear of the Nation). On July 11, 1963, police raided the farm and arrested several key figures of the ANC, including Govan Mbeki, Walter Sisulu, and others. Although Mandela was already in prison for earlier convictions related to his anti-apartheid activities, he was also brought to trial as a key figure in the organization's leadership.

The apartheid regime in South Africa, which institutionalized racial segregation and discrimination, sought to use the trial to crush the ANC and deter further resistance. The government charged the defendants under the Sabotage Act, accusing them of planning to violently overthrow the state, primarily through acts of sabotage rather than direct violence against people. This legal strategy was chosen to demonstrate that the accused were not merely political dissenters but dangerous insurgents.

The prosecution, led by Dr. Percy Yutar, presented evidence including documents seized during the raid, testimonies of state witnesses, and incriminating speeches. The defendants were accused of participating in activities aimed at inciting violence and disrupting vital services to bring about a revolutionary change in the government. The state's case was heavily bolstered by the discovery of Operation Mayibuye, a plan allegedly outlining a strategy for guerrilla warfare against the apartheid regime.

The defense, led by Bram Fischer, aimed to prove that the accused had pursued sabotage as a means to avoid a civil war and minimize loss of life. They argued that the ANC and Umkhonto we Sizwe had adopted sabotage as a last resort after all other forms of peaceful protest had been met with violent repression by the state. Mandela, representing himself and his co-defendants, delivered a powerful speech from the dock, known as the "I Am Prepared to Die" speech, in which he laid out the motivations behind their actions and their commitment to the struggle for a democratic and non-racial South Africa.

In his speech, Mandela articulated the philosophical and moral grounds of their resistance, emphasizing that the struggle was not against white people but against the oppressive system of apartheid. He detailed the systemic injustices faced by black South Africans, including poverty, lack of political rights, and the harsh restrictions of the pass laws. Mandela expressed his willingness to die for the cause, stating, "I have cherished the ideal of a democratic and free society in which all persons live together in harmony and with equal opportunities. It is an ideal which I hope to live for and to achieve. But if needs be, it is an ideal for which I am prepared to die."

The trial attracted global attention and condemnation. Many international observers, including prominent political figures, intellectuals, and organizations, criticized the apartheid regime and called for the release of the defendants. Despite the international outcry, the apartheid government pressed on with the trial, determined to secure a conviction and impose severe penalties.

On June 12, 1964, Judge Quartus de Wet delivered the verdict. While acknowledging the moral and political motivations behind the actions of the accused, he found them guilty of sabotage. However, instead of the death penalty, which many feared, the judge sentenced them to life imprisonment. This decision was seen as a compromise, possibly influenced by international pressure and the desire to avoid making the defendants martyrs.

Mandela and his co-defendants were sent to Robben Island, a notorious prison off the coast of Cape Town, where they were to spend the majority of their sentences. The harsh conditions of Robben Island, including forced labor, limited communication with the outside world, and restricted access to news and literature, were intended to break the spirits of the prisoners. However, Mandela and his fellow inmates used their time in prison to continue their political education and planning, strengthening their resolve to end apartheid.

The Rivonia Trial and the imprisonment of Mandela and other ANC leaders galvanized the anti-apartheid movement both within South Africa and internationally. It exposed the brutality and injustice of the apartheid system to a global audience, further isolating the South African government diplomatically and economically. The ANC and other liberation movements intensified their efforts, leading to increased activism, both domestically and abroad.

Mandela's imprisonment became a central focus of the international anti-apartheid campaign, symbolizing the broader struggle for freedom and equality in South Africa. Calls for his release became a rallying cry for activists worldwide, and the "Free Nelson Mandela" campaign gained widespread support, including from musicians, artists, and political leaders.

After 27 years in prison, Mandela was released on February 11, 1990, as part of a broader process of negotiations that led to the dismantling of apartheid. His release marked the beginning of a new era in South African history, culminating in the country's first multiracial democratic elections in 1994, in which Mandela was elected as South Africa's first black president.

The legacy of the Rivonia Trial is profound, symbolizing the struggle for justice and the triumph of resilience over oppression. Mandela's conduct during the trial and his subsequent years in prison highlighted his commitment to non-violence, reconciliation, and a vision of a South Africa free from racial discrimination. The trial stands as a testament to the power of moral courage and the enduring quest for human dignity and equality.

Today, the Rivonia Trial is remembered not only as a crucial moment in South Africa's history but also as a significant event in the global fight against racism and political oppression. The ideals expressed by Mandela during the trial continue to resonate, reminding us of the importance of standing up against injustice and advocating for a society where all individuals can live in freedom and peace.

Chapter 13: The Trial of Anne Boleyn

The trial of Anne Boleyn, the second wife of King Henry VIII of England, is a dramatic and tragic episode in English history, marked by political intrigue, personal vendettas, and the complexities of courtly life in the 16th century. Anne Boleyn's downfall and subsequent execution were significant not only because they involved the Queen of England but also because they had far-reaching implications for the English Reformation and the future of the Tudor dynasty.

Anne Boleyn's rise to prominence began in the early 1520s when she caught the eye of Henry VIII. Anne was known for her intelligence, charm, and wit, which distinguished her at court. Her relationship with Henry was controversial, not least because Henry was already married to Catherine of Aragon, with whom he had a daughter, Mary. Catherine's failure to produce a male heir had led Henry to seek an annulment of his marriage, a process complicated by the Pope's refusal to grant it due to political pressures, particularly from Catherine's nephew, Emperor Charles V of the Holy Roman Empire.

Anne Boleyn's role in Henry's quest for an annulment was pivotal. Her relationship with Henry spurred the king to take unprecedented steps, ultimately leading to the English Reformation. Unable to obtain a papal annulment, Henry broke with the Catholic Church and established the Church of England, with himself as the Supreme Head. This schism allowed him to annul his marriage to Catherine and marry Anne in 1533. Anne was crowned Queen Consort in June 1533, and shortly after, she gave birth to Elizabeth, who would later become one of England's greatest monarchs, Queen Elizabeth I. However, Anne's failure to provide Henry with a male heir and the political and personal enmities she garnered at court soon led to her downfall.

By 1536, Anne Boleyn's position had become increasingly precarious. Henry had grown frustrated with Anne's inability to produce a male heir, and Anne had made many enemies at court, including powerful figures such as Thomas Cromwell, Henry's chief minister, who had initially supported her but later turned against her. The reasons for Cromwell's change of heart are debated by historians, but it is likely that political and personal differences played a role. Cromwell may have viewed Anne as a threat to his influence over the king or as an obstacle to his broader political and religious reforms.

In May 1536, a series of charges were brought against Anne, including adultery, incest, and treason. The charges were based on allegations that Anne had engaged in sexual relationships with multiple men, including her own brother, George Boleyn, Viscount Rochford. Such accusations were highly scandalous and carried the penalty of death if proven. The speed and manner in which the charges were brought against Anne suggest that they were part of a deliberate plot to remove her from power, possibly orchestrated by Cromwell with Henry's tacit approval.

The trial of Anne Boleyn took place on May 15, 1536, at the Tower of London, before a specially convened court of peers, including her own uncle, the Duke of Norfolk. The trial was a spectacle of the Tudor judicial process, heavily influenced by the politics and personal animosities of the time. Anne was charged with committing adultery with several courtiers, including Henry Norris, Francis Weston, William Brereton, and Mark Smeaton, a musician. She was also accused of incest with her brother, George Boleyn, and conspiring to kill the king.

The evidence presented against Anne was largely circumstantial and based on dubious testimonies. Mark Smeaton, the only accused man to confess to the charges, did so under questionable circumstances, possibly coercion or torture. The other men steadfastly denied the accusations, as did Anne herself. During the trial, Anne eloquently defended herself, maintaining her innocence and highlighting the lack of concrete evidence against her. She argued that the charges were fabricated and that she was being persecuted because she had failed to provide Henry with a son.

Despite her defense, the outcome of the trial was likely predetermined. The court, composed of peers loyal to Henry and Cromwell, found Anne guilty on all charges. She was condemned to death, as were the men accused alongside her. George Boleyn, Norris, Weston, Brereton, and Smeaton were executed on May 17, 1536. Anne's execution was scheduled shortly thereafter, amid a backdrop of intense public and political scrutiny.

On May 19, 1536, Anne Boleyn was executed by beheading at the Tower of London. Her execution was carried out by a skilled French swordsman, brought over specifically for the purpose, which was considered a merciful method of execution compared to the axe. Before her death, Anne delivered a composed speech, expressing her loyalty to the king and resigning herself to her fate. Her final words and demeanor were recorded by contemporary chroniclers, who noted her courage and poise in the face of death.

The execution of Anne Boleyn had significant repercussions. It underscored the absolute power of the Tudor monarchy and the precarious nature of courtly life, where favor could be swiftly followed by disgrace. The fall of Anne Boleyn also marked a critical point in the English Reformation. Henry VIII's actions, including his marriage to Jane Seymour just days after Anne's execution, further solidified the break with Rome and the establishment of the Church of England.

Anne's legacy is complex and multifaceted. She is often remembered as a tragic figure, a victim of the political machinations of her time, and a woman who challenged the established norms of her society. Her daughter, Elizabeth I, would go on to become one of England's most celebrated monarchs, and in many ways, Anne's legacy was realized through Elizabeth's reign. The story of Anne Boleyn continues to captivate historians, writers, and the public, symbolizing the dramatic and often perilous life at the Tudor court.

Chapter 14: The Trial of Charles I

The trial of Charles I of England is one of the most significant events in British history, marking the first time a reigning monarch was legally tried and executed by his own subjects. This pivotal event occurred during the English Civil War, a conflict that pitted Royalist supporters of the king against Parliamentarians who sought to limit his powers. The trial and execution of Charles I not only brought an end to his reign but also had profound implications for the concept of monarchy, the rule of law, and the nature of governance in England.

Charles I ascended to the throne in 1625, inheriting a kingdom deeply divided by religious, political, and economic tensions. His reign was marked by a series of conflicts with Parliament over issues such as taxation, religious reforms, and the rights of subjects versus the authority of the crown. Charles's belief in the divine right of kings, which held that monarchs were answerable only to God and not to earthly authorities, often put him at odds with Parliament, which sought to assert its role in governance and to limit the king's arbitrary use of power.

The relationship between Charles I and Parliament deteriorated rapidly over the years, culminating in the outbreak of the English Civil War in 1642. The war was not merely a struggle for power but also a battle over fundamental principles of governance and individual rights. The Royalists, or Cavaliers, supported the king's authority, while the Parliamentarians, or Roundheads, opposed what they saw as his tyrannical rule. The conflict engulfed England, Scotland, and Ireland, resulting in significant loss of life and upheaval.

By 1646, after several years of fighting, the Parliamentarian forces, led by Oliver Cromwell and the New Model Army, had gained the upper hand. Charles I was captured and held prisoner, but negotiations for a settlement failed as he continued to maneuver for power and to seek alliances, including with the Scots. The king's refusal to make concessions, combined with fears of a royal resurgence, led to a hardening of attitudes among the Parliamentarian leadership.

In 1648, after a second civil war prompted by Charles's intrigues and support from Scottish forces, the Parliamentarians, now dominated by the more radical elements known as the Independents, decided that the king must be held accountable for the bloodshed and turmoil. This decision was unprecedented; traditionally, the monarchy was considered sacrosanct, and the idea of putting a king on trial was almost inconceivable.

Nevertheless, in December 1648, the House of Commons, purged of moderates and conservatives in what became known as Pride's Purge, resolved that Charles I should be brought to trial. The legal and political rationale for the trial was based on the belief that the king had betrayed the trust of the English people by waging war against them and attempting to re-establish absolute monarchy. The trial was also seen as a means to establish that even the monarch was not above the law and could be held accountable for his actions.

The trial of Charles I began on January 20, 1649, in Westminster Hall. It was conducted by a specially convened tribunal known as the High Court of Justice, composed of 135 commissioners, although only about 68 regularly attended. The presiding judge was John Bradshaw, a lawyer and member of Parliament. The charges against Charles included "treason and other high crimes," specifically that he had levied war against the Parliament and the people of England, thus violating the constitutional rights of his subjects.

Charles I's defense rested on his assertion of the divine right of kings. He refused to recognize the legitimacy of the court, arguing that no court had jurisdiction over a sovereign monarch. Charles contended that his authority came from God, not from the people or Parliament, and therefore he could not be lawfully tried by his own subjects. His refusal to plead or acknowledge the court's authority was a deliberate strategy to maintain his dignity and the principle of monarchy, even in the face of overwhelming opposition.

Despite his arguments, the trial proceeded. The prosecution, led by John Cook, presented evidence of Charles's actions during the civil war, including his military campaigns and negotiations with foreign powers. The aim was to demonstrate that the king had betrayed his duty to his people and sought to impose an arbitrary and tyrannical rule. The trial was also a public relations exercise, intended to justify the Parliamentarian cause and to delegitimize the monarchy as it had been practiced under Charles.

The outcome of the trial was never in doubt. On January 27, 1649, the court found Charles I guilty of treason and sentenced him to death. The sentence was met with mixed reactions; while some viewed it as a necessary act of justice and a step towards establishing a more just and lawful society, others saw it as a shocking and sacrilegious act against the divinely ordained monarchy.

Charles I was executed on January 30, 1649, outside the Banqueting House in Whitehall, London. His execution was a momentous and tragic event, witnessed by a large crowd. Before his death, Charles maintained his composure and dignity, addressing those present and reaffirming his belief in his divine right to rule. He was beheaded with a single stroke, and his death marked the end of the English monarchy, albeit temporarily.

The execution of Charles I was followed by the establishment of the Commonwealth of England, a republican government led by Oliver Cromwell and the Parliament. This period saw significant political and social changes, including the abolition of the monarchy and the House of Lords, and attempts at constitutional reform. However, the republic struggled with internal divisions and lacked widespread popular support, which eventually led to the restoration of the monarchy in 1660 under Charles II, Charles I's son.

The trial and execution of Charles I had profound and lasting implications. It challenged the traditional notion of monarchy and royal prerogative, setting a precedent for the accountability of rulers to the law and to their people. The event also highlighted the tension between the principles of absolute monarchy and emerging ideas of constitutionalism and popular sovereignty.

In the broader context of British and world history, the trial of Charles I is seen as a critical moment in the development of modern political thought and constitutional law. It raised fundamental questions about the nature of political authority, the rights of subjects, and the limits of power, which continued to influence political debates and developments in subsequent centuries.

The legacy of Charles I and his trial remains complex. While his execution was seen by some contemporaries as a necessary step to preserve liberty and justice, others viewed it as a martyrdom that paved the way for the excesses of Cromwell's rule. In the long term, the trial underscored the importance of rule of law, constitutional government, and the idea that even the highest authority is accountable to the people and the law. This legacy continues to resonate in modern discussions about governance, democracy, and the limits of power.

Chapter 15: The Trial of Oscar Wilde

The trial of Oscar Wilde, one of the most celebrated playwrights and poets of the late Victorian era, is a tragic and complex story that highlights the cultural and social mores of the time, as well as the devastating consequences of rigid societal norms and legal structures. Wilde's trials in 1895, on charges of "gross indecency" due to his homosexual relationships, not only led to his personal downfall but also marked a significant moment in the history of LGBTQ+ rights and the treatment of homosexuals under the law.

Oscar Wilde was born in 1854 in Dublin, Ireland, into a family of intellectuals. He gained fame in the late 19th century as a writer of novels, plays, and essays, known for his sharp wit, flamboyant style, and keen social commentary. Some of his most famous works include the novel "The Picture of Dorian Gray" and plays such as "The Importance of Being Earnest" and "An Ideal Husband." Wilde was a leading figure in the aesthetic movement, which advocated for "art for art's sake," and he was a prominent figure in London's cultural and social scene.

Wilde's downfall began with his relationship with Lord Alfred Douglas, a young poet and aristocrat. Douglas, often referred to as "Bosie," introduced Wilde to a circle of young men, many of whom were from lower social classes, with whom Wilde engaged in sexual relationships. These relationships, while known in certain circles, were dangerous given the legal and social climate of the time. Homosexual acts were criminalized under the Labouchere Amendment to the Criminal Law Amendment Act of 1885, which made "gross indecency" between men a punishable offense, carrying severe penalties including imprisonment and hard labor.

The events leading to Wilde's trials began with a feud between Wilde and Douglas's father, the Marquess of Queensberry. The Marquess, an outspoken and aggressive character, disapproved of the relationship between Wilde and his son. He attempted to publicly disgrace Wilde, culminating in an incident where he left a calling card at Wilde's club inscribed with the phrase "For Oscar Wilde, posing somdomite" (a misspelling of "sodomite"). Wilde, urged by Douglas and possibly motivated by a combination of outrage and a desire to defend his reputation, decided to sue the Marquess for criminal libel.

Wilde's decision to initiate legal proceedings was ill-advised. During the libel trial, which began on April 3, 1895, the Marquess's defense was that the accusation was true and thus not libelous. To prove this, the defense presented evidence of Wilde's relationships with various young men, many of whom were called to testify. Wilde's works and public statements were also scrutinized for evidence of immoral behavior. Under cross-examination by the Marquess's lawyer, Edward Carson, Wilde was asked about the nature of his relationships and whether he had engaged in inappropriate conduct. Wilde's responses, while clever and evasive, could not hide the reality of the situation. Faced with overwhelming evidence and to avoid a possible conviction for perjury, Wilde withdrew the case on April 5, 1895.

However, the withdrawal of the libel case was not the end of the matter. The evidence presented in the trial led to Wilde being arrested on charges of gross indecency. He was granted bail, but his initial attempt to flee the country was thwarted, partly due to indecision and the influence of friends and family. Wilde's first criminal trial began on April 26, 1895, with Sir Edward Clarke as his defense counsel. The trial was presided over by Justice Arthur Charles.

The prosecution, led by Charles Gill, focused on Wilde's relationships with young men, emphasizing the nature of these interactions and using testimonies from the young men involved, such as rent boys Alfred Wood and Edward Shelley, who provided explicit accounts of Wilde's conduct. The prosecution also presented letters from Wilde to Douglas, which were interpreted as evidence of romantic and sexual relationships. One letter, later published as "De

Profundis," was particularly incriminating due to its passionate language.

The defense's strategy was to argue that Wilde's relationships, while unconventional, did not amount to criminal behavior under the law. Wilde himself testified, maintaining his composure and employing his characteristic wit, but his performance on the stand was less confident than during the libel trial. The prosecution sought to undermine Wilde's credibility and morality, questioning him extensively about his works, letters, and associations.

The first trial ended with a hung jury, unable to reach a unanimous verdict. However, Wilde was not released; he was retried almost immediately, with the second trial commencing on May 21, 1895. This time, the presiding judge was Justice Wills, known for his harsh sentencing. The prosecution again presented the same evidence, but with greater vigor and emphasis on the seriousness of the charges.

During the second trial, Wilde's health and spirits visibly declined. The defense again called character witnesses and argued for acquittal on the grounds of insufficient evidence and the unreliability of the prosecution witnesses, many of whom were of questionable character and had admitted to blackmailing Wilde. Nevertheless, the atmosphere of the trial and public sentiment had turned decidedly against Wilde, influenced by the sensationalist press coverage and the social stigma attached to homosexuality.

On May 25, 1895, Wilde was convicted of gross indecency and sentenced to two years' hard labor. The severity of the sentence reflected both the letter of the law and the moral outrage of the Victorian public. Wilde was first imprisoned in Pentonville and then transferred to Wandsworth and later to Reading Gaol, where he suffered physically and mentally. The harsh conditions of prison life, including forced labor, poor diet, and isolation, severely impacted his health and well-being.

While in prison, Wilde wrote "De Profundis," a lengthy letter addressed to Douglas, reflecting on his life, trials, and the nature of suffering and redemption. This work, along with "The Ballad of Reading Gaol," composed after his release, provides deep insights into his inner turmoil and the profound sense of betrayal and despair he felt.

Wilde was released from prison on May 19, 1897, broken in health and spirit. He spent the remainder of his life in exile, primarily in France, under the name Sebastian Melmoth. During this period, Wilde lived in relative obscurity and poverty, supported by a small circle of friends. His relationship with Douglas, despite reconciliation attempts, remained strained. Wilde's final years were marked by declining health, largely due to the conditions endured during his imprisonment, and he died of meningitis on November 30, 1900, at the age of 46.

The trials of Oscar Wilde had lasting repercussions beyond his personal tragedy. They exposed the harsh realities of Victorian attitudes towards homosexuality and the legal and social penalties associated with it. Wilde's downfall was a public spectacle that highlighted the hypocrisies and moralistic fervor of the time. His case became a landmark in the history of LGBTQ+ rights, symbolizing the dangers of intolerance and the persecution of individuals based on their sexuality.

In the decades following his death, Wilde's reputation was rehabilitated, and he came to be celebrated not only for his literary genius but also as a symbol of artistic and personal freedom. His works, which critique the superficialities and contradictions of Victorian society, continue to be widely read and performed, appreciated for their wit, insight, and humanity. The legacy of Wilde's trials remains a poignant reminder of the societal prejudices and injustices faced by LGBTQ+ individuals and the enduring struggle for acceptance and equality.

Chapter 16: The Trial of Adolf Eichmann

The trial of Adolf Eichmann, one of the chief architects of the Holocaust, is a landmark event in international law, human rights, and the historical memory of the Holocaust. Eichmann, a high-ranking Nazi official, was captured in Argentina in 1960 by Israeli agents and subsequently brought to Israel to stand trial for his role in the systematic extermination of six million Jews during World War II. The trial, which took place in 1961, was a pivotal moment in the history of justice and accountability for crimes against humanity and had profound implications for how the world understands and responds to genocide.

Adolf Eichmann was born in 1906 in Solingen, Germany. He joined the Nazi Party in 1932 and quickly rose through the ranks of the SS, becoming one of the principal administrators of the Nazi regime's policies towards Jews. Eichmann's official title was head of the Jewish Affairs section of the Gestapo, a role in which he was responsible for the logistics of mass deportations of Jews to ghettos and extermination camps across Nazi-occupied Europe. Eichmann played a crucial role in the implementation of the "Final Solution," the Nazi plan to annihilate the Jewish population of Europe.

After the defeat of Nazi Germany in 1945, Eichmann evaded capture and went into hiding. He eventually fled to Argentina, where he lived under the alias Ricardo Klement. In 1960, Israeli intelligence agency Mossad tracked Eichmann down and, in a covert operation, kidnapped him and brought him to Israel. This action was controversial, as it involved violating Argentine sovereignty, but Israel justified it on the grounds of bringing a notorious war criminal to justice.

Eichmann's trial began on April 11, 1961, in Jerusalem. It was one of the first major trials to be widely televised, drawing international attention. The trial was presided over by three judges: Moshe Landau,

Benjamin Halevy, and Yitzhak Raveh. The chief prosecutor was Gideon Hausner, who faced the formidable task of prosecuting crimes of an unprecedented scale and horror. The trial was held in a newly constructed courtroom that could accommodate the large number of spectators and media representatives, underscoring the trial's significance as a public reckoning with the Holocaust.

The charges against Eichmann included crimes against humanity, war crimes, and crimes against the Jewish people. The prosecution aimed to demonstrate Eichmann's central role in the Nazi machinery of extermination, highlighting his responsibility for the deportation and murder of millions of Jews. The trial was not only about Eichmann's personal guilt but also served as an educational moment, bringing to light the full scale of the atrocities committed during the Holocaust.

One of the most powerful aspects of the trial was the testimony of Holocaust survivors, who for the first time publicly recounted their experiences in a judicial setting. These testimonies provided a harrowing and personal account of the suffering endured by millions and underscored the human impact of the crimes Eichmann was charged with. The survivors' stories covered the horrors of ghettos, mass shootings, concentration camps, and death marches, providing a comprehensive picture of the Nazi genocide.

Eichmann's defense strategy was largely based on the argument that he was merely following orders, a defense commonly referred to as the "Nuremberg Defense," after the Nuremberg Trials of major Nazi war criminals. Eichmann portrayed himself as a bureaucrat who did not personally harbor animosity towards Jews and claimed that he had no choice but to carry out orders from his superiors. He argued that he was a small cog in a vast machine, emphasizing the hierarchical nature of the Nazi state and suggesting that he lacked the authority to challenge the directives he was given.

However, the prosecution presented evidence that contradicted Eichmann's claims. Documents and testimonies showed that Eichmann was not only an enthusiastic implementer of the Final Solution but also took initiative in the planning and execution of mass deportations and killings. Eichmann's role in organizing the Wannsee Conference, where the Final Solution was formally outlined, was highlighted as evidence of his deep involvement in the genocidal policies. Moreover, his meticulous attention to detail in arranging transport and logistics for deportations demonstrated a level of commitment and initiative that went beyond merely following orders.

The trial also delved into the broader implications of Eichmann's actions and the nature of evil. Philosopher Hannah Arendt, who covered the trial for The New Yorker, famously coined the phrase "the banality of evil" to describe Eichmann. Arendt's observation pointed to the disturbing normalcy and bureaucratic detachment with which Eichmann carried out his duties, suggesting that extraordinary evil could be perpetrated by ordinary individuals performing their jobs without moral reflection.

The trial concluded on December 15, 1961, with Eichmann being found guilty on multiple counts, including crimes against humanity, war crimes, and crimes against the Jewish people. He was sentenced to death, a punishment carried out on June 1, 1962. Eichmann was hanged, and his body was cremated, with his ashes scattered at sea outside Israel's territorial waters to ensure that there would be no grave that could become a site of pilgrimage for neo-Nazis.

The trial of Adolf Eichmann had several far-reaching consequences. Firstly, it established a significant precedent for international law and the prosecution of war crimes and crimes against humanity. The trial demonstrated that individuals could be held accountable for atrocities, regardless of their position within a government or military hierarchy. It also underscored the principle that following orders is not a defense for committing gross human rights violations.

Secondly, the trial played a crucial role in Holocaust remembrance and education. The extensive media coverage and the public testimonies of survivors brought the horrors of the Holocaust into the global consciousness in a way that had not been achieved before. The trial's documentation of the genocide provided a detailed and irrefutable record of the events, countering Holocaust denial and ensuring that the memories of the victims would not be forgotten.

The trial also prompted a broader reflection on justice and morality. It raised questions about the nature of complicity, obedience, and individual responsibility in the face of state-sponsored atrocities. The discussions sparked by the trial contributed to a deeper understanding of how seemingly ordinary individuals can become perpetrators of mass violence and highlighted the importance of ethical reasoning in positions of authority.

Moreover, the trial had a significant impact on the Jewish community, both in Israel and globally. It provided a form of moral vindication and recognition for the suffering of Holocaust survivors and the Jewish people. It also reaffirmed the commitment of the State of Israel to seek justice for crimes committed against Jews, reinforcing the notion of Israel as a sanctuary for Jewish people worldwide.

In the decades since the trial, Adolf Eichmann's name has become synonymous with the machinery of the Holocaust and the dangers of uncritical obedience to authority. The trial continues to be studied in law schools, history courses, and ethics classes, serving as a critical case study in the pursuit of justice, the nature of evil, and the mechanisms of state power.

Chapter 17: The Trial of Sacco and Vanzetti

The trial of Sacco and Vanzetti, which took place in the 1920s, stands as one of the most controversial legal cases in American history, embodying the intense social and political tensions of the era. Nicola Sacco and Bartolomeo Vanzetti, both Italian immigrants and self-proclaimed anarchists, were accused of committing a robbery and double murder at the Slater and Morrill Shoe Company in South Braintree, Massachusetts, on April 15, 1920. The victims, a paymaster named Frederick Parmenter and a guard named Alessandro Berardelli, were shot and killed during the heist. Sacco and Vanzetti were arrested several days later, not for the murders initially, but for being in possession of anarchist literature and having firearms similar to those used in the crime.

The trial, which began in May 1921, quickly became a media sensation and a focal point of widespread international attention. The proceedings were marked by numerous irregularities and apparent biases. The presiding judge, Webster Thayer, exhibited open hostility toward the defendants, reportedly referring to them as "anarchist bastards" during the trial. The prosecution's case relied heavily on circumstantial evidence and eyewitness testimonies that were later deemed unreliable and contradictory. For instance, several witnesses could not positively identify Sacco and Vanzetti as the perpetrators, and some even retracted their statements, claiming they had been coerced or misled.

Despite the weak evidence, the jury found Sacco and Vanzetti guilty on July 14, 1921. Their conviction sparked outrage and widespread protests, as many believed the men were targeted for their political beliefs rather than any concrete evidence of their involvement in the crime. The case quickly became a symbol of the broader struggles against immigrant oppression and political repression in the United States. Prominent intellectuals, writers, and public figures, including Albert Einstein, H.G. Wells, and Felix Frankfurter, spoke out against the verdict and called for a retrial, arguing that the trial had been fundamentally unfair.

In the years following their conviction, numerous efforts were made to exonerate Sacco and Vanzetti. Legal appeals were repeatedly filed, but each was denied, and Governor Alvan T. Fuller of Massachusetts, after conducting a review of the case, upheld the verdict in 1927. This decision was met with even greater public outcry, and the execution date was set for August 23, 1927. In the days leading up to their execution, protests and demonstrations erupted around the world, with tens of thousands of people marching in cities such as Boston, New York, London, Paris, and Buenos Aires. Despite the massive public opposition, Sacco and Vanzetti were executed in the electric chair at Charlestown State Prison.

The aftermath of the trial left an indelible mark on American society. The execution of Sacco and Vanzetti is widely regarded as a miscarriage of justice, fueled by xenophobia, anti-immigrant sentiment, and political intolerance. Their case highlighted the deep divisions in American society and the extent to which prejudice and fear could influence the legal system. In the decades following their deaths, calls for a reassessment of their guilt continued, and the trial remained a subject of debate among historians, legal scholars, and social activists.

In 1977, on the 50th anniversary of their execution, Governor Michael Dukakis of Massachusetts issued a proclamation stating that Sacco and Vanzetti had been unfairly tried and convicted. While this proclamation did not exonerate them, it acknowledged the significant flaws in the trial and the lasting impact of their case on the American judicial system. The legacy of Sacco and Vanzetti endures as a poignant reminder of the dangers of prejudice and the importance of ensuring fairness and impartiality in the pursuit of justice. Their story continues to resonate as a powerful example of how legal and societal biases can lead to grave injustices and the ongoing struggle to protect the rights of all individuals, regardless of their background or beliefs.

Chapter 18: The Trial of Mary Queen of Scots

The trial of Mary Queen of Scots, which culminated in her execution in 1587, is one of the most dramatic and politically charged episodes in the history of the British monarchy. Mary Stuart, Queen of Scots, was born in 1542 and became queen when she was just six days old, following the death of her father, James V of Scotland. Her life was marked by a series of tumultuous events, alliances, and conflicts that ultimately led to her downfall.

Mary's early years were spent in France, where she was educated and married to the Dauphin Francis, who became King Francis II of France in 1559. Her time as Queen of France was brief, ending with Francis's death in 1560. Widowed and without a role in French politics, Mary returned to Scotland in 1561 to reclaim her throne. Her reign in Scotland was fraught with difficulties, including religious conflicts between Catholics and Protestants, as she herself was a devout Catholic in a country increasingly leaning toward Protestantism. Her marriage to Henry Stuart, Lord Darnley, in 1565 was intended to strengthen her position, but it only added to her troubles. Darnley was unpopular, and their relationship deteriorated quickly. The situation reached a crisis point when Darnley was murdered in 1567, an event that many suspected Mary of being involved in, although evidence to prove her guilt was lacking. Her subsequent marriage to James Hepburn, Earl of Bothwell, who was widely believed to have orchestrated Darnley's murder, led to widespread outrage and rebellion among the Scottish nobility.

Faced with insurrection, Mary was forced to abdicate the throne in favor of her infant son, James VI, and she fled to England seeking protection from her cousin, Queen Elizabeth I. Elizabeth, however, saw Mary as a significant threat to her own throne. Mary's claim to the

English crown, through her grandmother Margaret Tudor, was seen by many Catholics as legitimate, particularly since Elizabeth was perceived as a Protestant usurper by Catholic factions. Elizabeth's advisors, especially Sir Francis Walsingham, were deeply suspicious of Mary and believed she was involved in numerous Catholic plots to overthrow Elizabeth and seize the English throne.

Mary was placed under house arrest, but her confinement did little to curb her ambitions or conspiracies. Over the years, she became the focal point of various Catholic plots against Elizabeth, the most significant being the Babington Plot of 1586. This conspiracy, orchestrated by Anthony Babington, aimed to assassinate Elizabeth and place Mary on the throne. Through intercepted letters and intelligence work by Walsingham's spy network, Mary's complicity in the plot was uncovered. The discovery of the Babington Plot provided the evidence Elizabeth needed to take drastic action against her rival.

Mary was put on trial in October 1586 at Fotheringhay Castle. The trial was a politically charged affair, with Elizabeth's government determined to secure a conviction. Mary, despite her royal status, was denied many legal rights, including access to legal counsel and the opportunity to review evidence against her. She defended herself with dignity, denying any involvement in the plot to kill Elizabeth and arguing that she had been unjustly accused. Despite her protestations, the outcome of the trial was never in doubt. Mary was found guilty of treason, and Elizabeth, after much hesitation, signed her death warrant.

On February 8, 1587, Mary was executed at Fotheringhay Castle. Her execution was a somber and controversial event. Dressed in a crimson gown, symbolizing her Catholic martyrdom, Mary faced her death with remarkable composure. Her final moments were marked by her prayer and a calm acceptance of her fate. The execution itself was gruesome; the executioner's initial blow missed her neck, and it took two more strokes to complete the act. Mary's death sent shockwaves through Europe, particularly in Catholic countries, where she was seen as a martyr for her faith. It also solidified Elizabeth's position, eliminating a significant threat to her reign but at the cost of executing a fellow queen, an act that haunted her for the rest of her life.

Mary's trial and execution have been the subject of extensive historical debate and analysis. Many view her as a victim of political machinations and religious conflict, caught in the crossfire of the power struggle between Catholicism and Protestantism in Europe. Her tragic fate underscores the precarious nature of royal power and the lengths to which rulers would go to secure their thrones. The legacy of Mary Queen of Scots continues to fascinate historians, writers, and the public, symbolizing the enduring conflict between personal ambition, religious faith, and political necessity in the tumultuous world of 16th-century Europe.

Chapter 19: The Trial of Al Capone

The trial of Al Capone, one of the most infamous gangsters in American history, marked a pivotal moment in the struggle against organized crime during the early 20th century. Alphonse Gabriel Capone, better known as Al Capone, rose to prominence during the Prohibition era, when the manufacture, sale, and transportation of alcoholic beverages were banned in the United States. Capone capitalized on this nationwide prohibition, building a vast criminal empire centered in Chicago. His syndicate was involved in various illicit activities, including bootlegging, gambling, prostitution, and racketeering, making Capone one of the wealthiest and most powerful figures in the underworld.

Born in Brooklyn, New York, in 1899 to Italian immigrant parents, Capone's early life was marked by a series of run-ins with the law. By his early twenties, he had moved to Chicago and began working for Johnny Torrio, a leading figure in the city's underworld. When Torrio retired after an assassination attempt, Capone took over his operations, quickly expanding the reach and influence of the organization. Capone's reign in Chicago was characterized by ruthless violence, with numerous gang wars and assassinations marking his tenure. The most notorious of these was the St. Valentine's Day Massacre in 1929, where seven members of a rival gang were gunned down in a brutal attack that shocked the nation. Despite widespread suspicion of his involvement, Capone managed to evade direct criminal charges due to his ability to manipulate and intimidate witnesses and law enforcement officials.

Capone's ostentatious lifestyle and brazen defiance of the law made him a prime target for federal authorities. The U.S. government, under the leadership of President Herbert Hoover, was determined to bring him to justice. With Capone's criminal activities largely shielded from prosecution due to corruption and fear, federal agents, including the dedicated efforts of Eliot Ness and his "Untouchables," focused on a different angle: tax evasion. Despite his vast wealth and public displays of affluence, Capone had never filed an income tax return, a fact that would become his Achilles' heel.

The federal government's strategy to convict Capone on tax evasion charges was masterminded by Assistant Attorney General Mabel Walker Willebrandt and led by Frank J. Wilson, an agent of the Internal Revenue Service's Intelligence Unit. Wilson meticulously pieced together evidence of Capone's income from his illegal activities, using informants, ledger books, and testimonies from former associates. The investigation uncovered substantial unreported income, setting the stage for Capone's indictment in June 1931.

Capone was charged with 22 counts of tax evasion and faced trial in the U.S. District Court in Chicago. The trial began on October 6, 1931, and was presided over by Judge James Herbert Wilkerson. From the outset, the government took extensive precautions to ensure the trial's integrity, given Capone's reputation for bribery and intimidation. Judge Wilkerson made the unprecedented move of switching the jury at the last moment to prevent any tampering, a decision that likely played a crucial role in the trial's outcome.

Throughout the trial, the prosecution, led by U.S. Attorney George E.Q. Johnson, presented a compelling case against Capone. They detailed his lavish expenditures and lifestyle, contrasting it with his meager declared income. Witnesses included bookkeepers and accountants who testified about Capone's financial transactions and the elaborate methods used to hide his profits. Capone's defense, led by attorney Michael Ahern, attempted to argue that Capone's income was exaggerated and that the government lacked concrete proof linking him directly to the income streams in question. However, the defense was unable to counter the overwhelming documentary evidence and the testimonies of credible witnesses.

On October 17, 1931, after nine hours of deliberation, the jury returned a guilty verdict on five counts of tax evasion. Capone was sentenced to 11 years in federal prison, fined $50,000, and charged $7,692 in court costs, along with $215,000 plus interest for back taxes. The sentence was the harshest ever imposed for tax evasion at the time, reflecting the government's determination to make an example of Capone.

Capone began serving his sentence at the Cook County Jail before being transferred to the U.S. Penitentiary in Atlanta, Georgia. However, due to concerns about his ability to influence prison officials and continue his criminal activities, he was eventually moved to the newly opened Alcatraz Federal Penitentiary in San Francisco Bay in 1934. Alcatraz, known for its maximum security and isolation, ensured that Capone was cut off from his criminal network. During his incarceration, Capone's health deteriorated significantly, largely due to untreated syphilis, which led to paresis, a severe neurological condition.

Capone was released from prison in 1939 after serving seven years, primarily due to his failing health. He spent his remaining years in relative obscurity at his mansion in Palm Island, Florida, and died in 1947 from cardiac arrest following a stroke. The trial and conviction of Al Capone had a profound impact on law enforcement and the fight against organized crime in America. It demonstrated the effectiveness of targeting the financial aspects of criminal enterprises and laid the groundwork for future investigations and prosecutions of high-profile criminals. Capone's downfall marked the end of an era in Chicago's underworld and signaled a shift in the federal government's approach to combating organized crime.

The trial also highlighted the challenges and limitations of the legal system in addressing complex and entrenched criminal organizations. While Capone's conviction was a significant victory, it did not eradicate organized crime, which adapted and evolved in response to increased law enforcement efforts. Nevertheless, the trial of Al Capone remains a landmark case in American legal history, illustrating the power of persistent and strategic law enforcement in bringing even the most formidable criminals to justice.

Chapter 20: The Trial of Aaron Burr

The trial of Aaron Burr is one of the most intriguing and complex episodes in American history, reflecting the turbulent political landscape of the early republic. Aaron Burr, a former Vice President of the United States, was charged with treason in 1807, accused of plotting to create an independent nation by seizing land in the western territories of the United States and Spanish-held territories in North America. This trial not only highlighted the fragile nature of the young American republic but also underscored the intense personal and political rivalries of the era.

Aaron Burr was born in 1756 in Newark, New Jersey, into a prominent family; his father was a co-founder of the College of New Jersey, now Princeton University, and his grandfather was the famous theologian, Jonathan Edwards. Burr had a distinguished career as a Revolutionary War officer and later as a lawyer and politician. He served as a U.S. Senator from New York and became the third Vice President of the United States under President Thomas Jefferson. Burr's tenure as Vice President is best remembered for his deadly duel with Alexander Hamilton in 1804. The duel, which resulted in Hamilton's death, effectively ended Burr's political career and made him a controversial figure.

After his term as Vice President ended in 1805, Burr's ambitions did not wane. He embarked on a venture that would lead to his trial for treason. Burr began recruiting supporters for a grand, albeit vague, scheme. He envisioned leading a group of settlers to the western territories, where he would establish a new independent nation. His exact intentions remain a subject of historical debate. Some believe Burr aimed to create an empire in the West, possibly including Mexico, while others think he merely sought to settle lands legally acquired. Nevertheless, Burr's plans involved significant military preparations and clandestine meetings, raising suspicions among federal authorities.

One of Burr's key associates was General James Wilkinson, the Governor of the Louisiana Territory and a highly controversial figure. Wilkinson was a double agent, simultaneously serving the United States and Spain. Burr and Wilkinson's correspondence, particularly a letter in code from Burr outlining his plans, became crucial evidence in the treason charges against Burr. Wilkinson, fearing exposure and seeking to protect himself, betrayed Burr by sending the letter to President Jefferson, along with a warning about Burr's alleged conspiracy.

In 1806, President Jefferson issued a proclamation calling for the arrest of anyone involved in illegal military expeditions against Spanish territories, specifically targeting Burr's activities. Burr was arrested in early 1807 in Alabama and brought to Richmond, Virginia, for trial. The legal proceedings against Burr were highly publicized and politically charged, with President Jefferson taking a keen interest in ensuring Burr's conviction. This unprecedented involvement of a sitting president in a criminal trial highlighted the political stakes and personal animosities underlying the case.

Burr was charged with treason under Article III, Section 3 of the U.S. Constitution, which defines treason as levying war against the United States or adhering to their enemies, giving them aid and comfort. The trial began in August 1807, presided over by Chief Justice John Marshall, who was also Jefferson's distant cousin and political rival. Marshall's role in the trial was critical, as his legal interpretations would shape the outcome.

The prosecution faced significant challenges in proving that Burr had committed an overt act of treason, as required by the Constitution. Treason required not just intent but an actual act of levying war against the United States, witnessed by two people. The prosecution, led by U.S. Attorney George Hay, argued that Burr's assembling of armed men on Blennerhassett Island in the Ohio River constituted an overt act of war. However, the defense, led by prominent attorneys Edmund

Randolph and Luther Martin, contended that no actual act of war had occurred and that Burr's activities, while potentially conspiratorial, did not meet the constitutional definition of treason.

Throughout the trial, Burr maintained his innocence, asserting that his intentions had been misinterpreted and that his actions did not amount to treason. Chief Justice Marshall's rulings during the trial were pivotal. Marshall insisted on a strict interpretation of the Constitution's treason clause, requiring clear evidence of an overt act of war. He ruled that mere conspiracy or intent was insufficient for a treason conviction. This stringent standard of proof made it difficult for the prosecution to secure a conviction.

One of the most dramatic moments of the trial came when Marshall subpoenaed President Jefferson to produce documents related to the case. Jefferson refused, citing executive privilege and arguing that he was not subject to ordinary judicial processes. This standoff between the judiciary and the executive branch underscored the separation of powers and set an important precedent for future interactions between the branches of government.

Ultimately, the jury acquitted Burr of treason on September 1, 1807. They concluded that the evidence presented did not meet the constitutional standard for treason, as no overt act of levying war had been proven. Burr was also acquitted of a lesser charge of high misdemeanor, related to his alleged plans to attack Spanish territories. Despite his acquittal, Burr's reputation was irreparably damaged, and he lived the rest of his life in relative obscurity, facing financial difficulties and diminished political influence.

The trial of Aaron Burr remains a landmark case in American legal history, illustrating the complexities of the early republic and the challenges of defining and prosecuting treason. It highlighted the delicate balance between national security and individual rights, the importance of judicial independence, and the potential for political rivalries to influence legal proceedings. The trial also reinforced the necessity of adhering to constitutional principles, even in cases involving high-profile figures and alleged threats to national stability.

In the broader context of American history, Burr's trial underscores the enduring tensions between ambition, legality, and loyalty in the nation's political landscape. It serves as a reminder of the high stakes involved in the early republic's efforts to establish and maintain a stable and lawful government amidst internal and external challenges. The case continues to be studied and debated by historians, legal scholars, and those interested in the intricate interplay of law, politics, and personal ambition in the formation of the United States.

Chapter 21: The Trial of Emmett Till's Murderers

The trial of the murderers of Emmett Till in 1955 is a seminal event in American history, highlighting the profound racial injustices of the time and igniting a spark in the Civil Rights Movement. Emmett Till, a 14-year-old African American boy from Chicago, was visiting relatives in Money, Mississippi, during the summer of 1955. His brutal murder, and the subsequent trial of his accused killers, Roy Bryant and J.W. Milam, exposed the depth of racial hatred and the failings of the legal system in the South.

Emmett Till's tragic story began when he reportedly whistled at Carolyn Bryant, a white woman, in a local grocery store. Accounts of the interaction vary, but the incident itself, minor as it was, breached the rigid racial codes of the Jim Crow South. A few days later, on August 28, 1955, Roy Bryant, Carolyn's husband, and his half-brother, J.W. Milam, abducted Till from his great-uncle Mose Wright's home in the middle of the night. They brutally beat him, gouged out one of his eyes, shot him in the head, and then disposed of his body in the Tallahatchie River, weighing it down with a 70-pound cotton gin fan tied around his neck with barbed wire. Till's body was so disfigured that it could only be identified by a ring he was wearing, which belonged to his father.

When Till's body was recovered three days later, the news of his murder spread quickly. His mother, Mamie Till-Mobley, made the courageous decision to have an open-casket funeral in Chicago, allowing the world to see the brutality inflicted on her son. The images of Till's mutilated body, published in Jet magazine and other outlets, shocked and horrified the nation, bringing unprecedented attention to the violent realities of racial segregation and injustice in the United States.

The trial of Roy Bryant and J.W. Milam for Till's murder took place in September 1955 in Sumner, Mississippi. The case was tried in a segregated courthouse, with an all-white, all-male jury, reflecting the deep-seated racial biases of the time. The defense attorneys, Sidney Carlton and J.J. Breland, capitalized on these prejudices, portraying Bryant and Milam as protectors of white womanhood and playing to the jurors' racist sentiments. The trial proceedings were a spectacle, with the courtroom packed with reporters, civil rights activists, and local residents. The defense's strategy included questioning the identity of Till's body and suggesting that the NAACP had planted the corpse to stir up trouble.

Despite overwhelming evidence against the defendants, including eyewitness testimony from Mose Wright, who bravely identified Bryant and Milam as the men who had taken Till from his home, the trial was marred by blatant racism. Wright's testimony was particularly significant; it was rare and dangerous for a black man to accuse white men in a Southern court at that time. Other witnesses corroborated the presence of Till at Bryant's store and his subsequent abduction. However, the defense sought to discredit these accounts and cast doubt on the prosecution's case.

The jury deliberated for just over an hour before returning a verdict of not guilty. One juror later remarked that they would have reached a decision even sooner had they not taken a break to drink soda. The acquittal of Bryant and Milam was met with outrage and disbelief by those outside the segregated South, but it was hardly surprising to those familiar with the entrenched racism and injustice in Mississippi. Following the trial, Bryant and Milam brazenly admitted to the murder in an interview with Look magazine, confident that they could not be retried due to double jeopardy laws.

The trial's outcome and the public confession of the murderers underscored the systemic racism within the American legal system and society at large. The acquittal of Bryant and Milam highlighted the pervasive power of white supremacy and the lengths to which it would go to protect itself. The blatant miscarriage of justice in Emmett Till's case became a rallying point for the Civil Rights Movement, galvanizing activists and ordinary citizens alike to push for change.

The impact of Till's murder and the trial was profound and far-reaching. Civil rights leaders like Rosa Parks, who later said that Till's murder was on her mind when she refused to give up her seat on a Montgomery bus, were deeply influenced by the case. The public outcry helped to mobilize support for subsequent efforts to challenge segregation and discrimination. The images of Till's body and the story of his brutal murder served as stark reminders of the urgent need for civil rights reform and the eradication of racial violence.

In the decades following the trial, Emmett Till's case has remained a powerful symbol of racial injustice. Efforts to reopen the case and achieve some measure of justice continued, although legal and societal obstacles persisted. In 2004, the U.S. Department of Justice reopened the investigation into Till's murder, and his body was exhumed for an autopsy. However, no new charges were brought against the original defendants, both of whom had since died. In 2017, Carolyn Bryant, now Carolyn Bryant Donham, admitted that she had fabricated parts of her testimony, further underscoring the miscarriage of justice.

Emmett Till's legacy endures as a poignant reminder of the brutal realities of racism and the struggle for justice and equality. His story continues to inspire activism and education, emphasizing the importance of confronting and challenging systemic racism. The trial of his murderers stands as a stark example of the failures of the American legal system and the necessity of continued efforts to achieve true justice and civil rights for all.

Chapter 22: The Trial of Edward Snowden

The trial of Edward Snowden, while yet to take place in a physical courtroom, is an ongoing legal and political saga that has captivated the world since 2013. Snowden, a former National Security Agency (NSA) contractor, leaked classified information revealing extensive global surveillance programs operated by the NSA and its international partners. This disclosure prompted a global debate on privacy, security, and the reach of government power in the digital age. The potential trial of Edward Snowden, if he were to return to the United States, would be one of the most significant legal proceedings in contemporary history, touching upon issues of national security, whistleblower protection, and the public's right to know.

Edward Joseph Snowden was born on June 21, 1983, in Elizabeth City, North Carolina. He grew up in a family with a strong government service background. His grandfather, a rear admiral in the U.S. Coast Guard, later became a senior official with the FBI and was at the Pentagon on September 11, 2001. This familial background deeply influenced Snowden, who joined the U.S. Army Reserve in 2004, hoping to serve his country. However, he was discharged after breaking both of his legs during a training accident. Undeterred, Snowden pursued a career in intelligence, eventually securing positions with the Central Intelligence Agency (CIA) and later as a contractor for the NSA.

Snowden's disillusionment with the extent of government surveillance grew over time. While working at an NSA office in Hawaii, he became increasingly disturbed by the agency's programs, which he believed infringed on the privacy of American citizens and people worldwide. In early 2013, Snowden made the momentous decision to leak a vast cache of classified documents to journalists

Glenn Greenwald, Laura Poitras, and Ewen MacAskill. These documents revealed the scope of NSA's surveillance operations, including the collection of phone records from millions of Americans, the PRISM program which allowed direct access to the systems of major internet companies, and the collaboration with foreign governments in mass surveillance.

The first disclosures, published by The Guardian and The Washington Post in June 2013, sent shockwaves through governments and the public alike. They revealed that the NSA had been secretly collecting the telephony metadata of millions of Verizon customers under a court order issued by the Foreign Intelligence Surveillance Court (FISC). This was followed by revelations of the PRISM program, which showed the NSA had access to data from companies such as Google, Facebook, Apple, and Microsoft. These disclosures painted a picture of a surveillance apparatus far more expansive than previously known.

The U.S. government responded swiftly and aggressively. Snowden was charged with theft of government property, unauthorized communication of national defense information, and willful communication of classified communications intelligence information to an unauthorized person, under the Espionage Act of 1917. These charges collectively carry a potential prison sentence of up to 30 years. The U.S. government also revoked Snowden's passport, effectively stranding him in Hong Kong, where he had initially fled. From there, he sought asylum in various countries, eventually finding temporary refuge in Russia, where he was granted asylum and later residency.

Snowden's revelations sparked a global debate on the balance between national security and individual privacy. Supporters hailed him as a whistleblower and a hero who exposed the overreach of government surveillance and sparked necessary reforms. Critics, however, labeled him a traitor who had endangered national security and jeopardized the safety of intelligence personnel and operations.

The impact of Snowden's leaks was profound, leading to significant legal and policy changes in several countries.

In the United States, the leaks led to the introduction of the USA FREEDOM Act, which aimed to end the bulk collection of American phone records under Section 215 of the Patriot Act. This legislation, signed into law by President Barack Obama in June 2015, represented the most significant curtailment of U.S. government surveillance powers since the 1970s. Internationally, Snowden's disclosures prompted many countries to reassess their own surveillance laws and practices, leading to reforms and increased scrutiny of intelligence agencies.

Despite the far-reaching consequences of his actions, Snowden has remained in Russia, aware that returning to the United States would likely result in his arrest and prosecution under the Espionage Act. His legal team has argued that he should be allowed to present a public interest defense, arguing that his disclosures were in the interest of transparency and democratic accountability. However, under current U.S. law, the Espionage Act does not provide for a public interest defense, meaning that Snowden would likely be unable to argue that his actions were justified by their societal benefits.

Snowden has continued to advocate for privacy and civil liberties from his place of exile. He published a memoir, "Permanent Record," in 2019, in which he recounts his life, motivations, and the process of leaking the classified documents. His story has been the subject of numerous books, documentaries, and films, further cementing his status as a pivotal figure in the discourse on privacy and government surveillance.

The question of whether Snowden should be pardoned or allowed to return to the United States without facing charges remains a contentious issue. Some politicians and public figures have called for clemency, arguing that Snowden's actions, while illegal, were morally justified and have led to necessary reforms. Others maintain that he should face justice for his unauthorized disclosure of classified information, which they argue compromised national security.

In August 2020, President Donald Trump stated that he would look into the possibility of pardoning Snowden, but no formal action was taken before the end of his term. The Biden administration has not indicated any significant departure from the previous stance on Snowden's legal status, leaving his future uncertain.

The potential trial of Edward Snowden, should he ever return to the United States, would undoubtedly be a landmark case. It would raise fundamental questions about the role of whistleblowers in a democratic society, the limits of governmental transparency, and the balance between national security and individual rights. The outcome of such a trial could set significant precedents for how whistleblowers are treated and how state secrets are managed in an era of digital information.

Snowden's case continues to resonate globally, symbolizing the complex interplay between surveillance, privacy, and freedom in the modern world. His actions have irrevocably changed the way people think about their digital footprints and the extent to which their governments monitor their activities. The debates ignited by his disclosures are likely to persist for many years, reflecting the ongoing struggle to balance security and liberty in a rapidly evolving technological landscape.

Chapter 23: The Trial of the Chicago Seven

The Trial of the Chicago Seven is one of the most significant and dramatic legal battles in American history, symbolizing the deep political and cultural divisions of the late 1960s. Originally known as the Chicago Eight, this group of anti-Vietnam War activists faced charges of conspiracy and incitement to riot, stemming from the violent clashes between protesters and police during the 1968 Democratic National Convention in Chicago. The trial, which took place from September 1969 to February 1970, became a focal point for the broader societal conflict over the Vietnam War, civil rights, and the counterculture movement.

The defendants, later known as the Chicago Seven after the case against Bobby Seale was separated, included Abbie Hoffman, Jerry Rubin, Tom Hayden, Rennie Davis, David Dellinger, John Froines, and Lee Weiner. These individuals were prominent activists from various political backgrounds, united by their opposition to the Vietnam War and their commitment to social change. The original group of eight also included Bobby Seale, co-founder of the Black Panther Party, whose trial was severed due to his disruptive behavior and the judge's decision to try him separately.

The events leading to the trial began in August 1968, when tens of thousands of protesters gathered in Chicago to demonstrate against the Vietnam War and the Democratic Party's support for it. The protests were organized by a coalition of groups, including the National Mobilization Committee to End the War in Vietnam (MOBE), the Youth International Party (Yippies), and Students for a Democratic Society (SDS). The protesters faced a heavily militarized police force, ordered by Chicago Mayor Richard J. Daley to maintain order at all costs. The confrontations between protesters and police turned violent, with widespread reports of police brutality, resulting in hundreds of injuries and arrests.

The federal government, under President Lyndon B. Johnson and later President Richard Nixon, decided to prosecute the leaders of the protest under the newly enacted Anti-Riot Act, part of the Civil Rights Act of 1968, which made it a federal crime to cross state lines with the intent to incite a riot. This decision was widely seen as an attempt to stifle dissent and criminalize political protest. The indictment, issued in March 1969, charged the defendants with conspiracy to incite a riot and with individual acts of crossing state lines with the intent to incite a riot.

The trial began in the U.S. District Court for the Northern District of Illinois, presided over by Judge Julius Hoffman. From the outset, the trial was marked by a contentious and often chaotic atmosphere. The defendants, particularly Abbie Hoffman and Jerry Rubin, frequently clashed with Judge Hoffman and the prosecution, led by U.S. Attorney Thomas Foran and Assistant U.S. Attorney Richard Schultz. The defendants' legal team, which included prominent civil rights lawyer William Kunstler and attorney Leonard Weinglass, argued that the charges were politically motivated and that the defendants were being prosecuted for their beliefs and their opposition to the Vietnam War.

One of the most dramatic and controversial aspects of the trial involved Bobby Seale. Seale, who had been denied the right to choose his own attorney and was instead represented by Kunstler and Weinglass, repeatedly disrupted the proceedings by insisting on his right to represent himself. His vocal objections and confrontations with Judge Hoffman led to him being bound, gagged, and chained to a chair in the courtroom, a shocking image that underscored the trial's highly charged nature. Eventually, Judge Hoffman declared a mistrial in Seale's case, and he was sentenced to four years in prison for contempt of court, later overturned on appeal.

Throughout the trial, the defense sought to highlight the political nature of the charges and the broader context of the antiwar movement. They called a range of witnesses, including cultural figures like Allen Ginsberg and Arlo Guthrie, and sought to demonstrate that the protests were largely peaceful until provoked by police violence. The prosecution, on the other hand, focused on the alleged plans and actions of the defendants, attempting to portray them as dangerous radicals intent on inciting violence.

The trial was characterized by numerous moments of high drama and surrealism. Abbie Hoffman and Jerry Rubin, known for their theatrical and confrontational style, often mocked the court proceedings, at one point showing up in judicial robes and blowing kisses to the jury. Judge Hoffman's handling of the trial was widely criticized as biased and overly harsh; he frequently clashed with the defense attorneys, issued numerous contempt citations, and imposed strict limitations on the defense's ability to present its case.

In February 1970, after a trial that lasted more than four months, the jury returned its verdict. Five of the defendants—Abbie Hoffman, Jerry Rubin, Tom Hayden, Rennie Davis, and David Dellinger—were found guilty of crossing state lines with intent to incite a riot. John Froines and Lee Weiner were acquitted of all charges. The five convicted defendants were sentenced to five years in prison and fined $5,000 each. However, the convictions were overturned on appeal in 1972 by the U.S. Court of Appeals for the Seventh Circuit, which cited errors by Judge Hoffman and the exclusion of evidence favorable to the defense. The court also noted the judge's evident bias against the defendants and their attorneys.

The trial of the Chicago Seven had a lasting impact on American society and the legal system. It highlighted the deep political and cultural divides of the 1960s, with the courtroom becoming a microcosm of the broader conflicts over the Vietnam War, civil rights, and the counterculture movement. The trial also raised important questions about the limits of free speech and the right to protest, as well as the role of the judiciary in adjudicating politically charged cases.

The trial also served as a catalyst for change within the legal profession and the broader justice system. The aggressive tactics used by the prosecution and the judge's handling of the trial prompted calls for reforms to ensure greater fairness and impartiality in politically sensitive cases. The case also underscored the importance of the right to a fair trial and the need for judges to maintain neutrality and avoid political biases.

In the years since the trial, the story of the Chicago Seven has continued to resonate in American culture. The trial has been the subject of numerous books, documentaries, and films, most recently Aaron Sorkin's 2020 film "The Trial of the Chicago 7," which brought renewed attention to the case and its historical significance. The film dramatizes the events of the trial and explores its themes of political protest, justice, and the enduring struggle for civil rights.

The legacy of the Chicago Seven trial is a testament to the power of dissent and the importance of protecting the right to protest in a democratic society. It serves as a reminder of the need to remain vigilant against attempts to suppress political expression and the importance of upholding the principles of justice and equality. As the United States continues to grapple with issues of political polarization, civil rights, and the role of protest in effecting social change, the trial of the Chicago Seven remains a powerful symbol of the enduring struggle for justice and the right to dissent.

Chapter 24: The Trial of the Guildford Four

The Trial of the Guildford Four is a significant and harrowing chapter in the history of British justice, emblematic of the dangers of wrongful convictions and the miscarriages of justice that can occur under the pressure of public and political demands. The case involved the wrongful imprisonment of four individuals—Gerry Conlon, Paul Hill, Patrick Armstrong, and Carole Richardson—who were accused of carrying out bombings in Guildford and Woolwich on behalf of the Irish Republican Army (IRA) during a particularly violent period of the Northern Ireland conflict known as "The Troubles."

The events that led to the trial began on October 5, 1974, when two bombs exploded in pubs in Guildford, Surrey, killing five people and injuring more than sixty others. These bombings, along with another attack in Woolwich a month later, heightened public fear and anger, prompting a vigorous response from the British government and law enforcement agencies desperate to find the perpetrators. The climate of fear and the demand for swift justice set the stage for the subsequent miscarriages of justice.

In the aftermath of the bombings, the police quickly arrested the four young individuals who became known as the Guildford Four. Gerry Conlon, Paul Hill, Patrick Armstrong, and Carole Richardson were young, and some had connections to Northern Ireland, making them convenient targets for a police force under immense pressure to produce results. The investigation and subsequent interrogations were marked by severe irregularities and abuses. The Guildford Four were subjected to intense and prolonged questioning, during which they were physically and psychologically abused. The interrogations led to coerced confessions, which became the cornerstone of the prosecution's case against them.

The trial took place at the Old Bailey in London in 1975. Despite the lack of forensic evidence linking the four to the bombings, the confessions obtained under duress were enough to secure their convictions. The prosecution argued that the four were part of an IRA bombing campaign, and the confessions, though later retracted, were presented as irrefutable proof of their guilt. The defense struggled to counter the weight of the confessions, and the atmosphere of the time, marked by fear of IRA violence, played a significant role in swaying the jury.

On October 22, 1975, the Guildford Four were found guilty of murder and sentenced to life imprisonment. The verdicts were met with relief by the public and the authorities, who saw the convictions as a victory in the fight against terrorism. However, doubts about the fairness of the trial and the reliability of the evidence began to surface almost immediately. The case against the Guildford Four was further complicated by the wrongful convictions of another group of individuals known as the Maguire Seven, who were accused of providing bomb-making materials to the IRA. Among the Maguire Seven were Gerry Conlon's father, Giuseppe Conlon, and other members of the Maguire family. Their trial, which took place shortly after the Guildford Four's, was also marked by dubious evidence and unfair procedures, resulting in additional miscarriages of justice.

Over the years, significant evidence emerged that cast doubt on the convictions of the Guildford Four. In 1977, a detailed confession by an IRA member, Paul Michael Hill, implicating other individuals in the bombings was ignored by the authorities. Additionally, the forensic evidence presented at the trials of the Guildford Four and the Maguire Seven was later discredited. Despite these developments, it took many years of persistent campaigning by the families of the convicted, along with legal advocates and human rights organizations, to bring about a reevaluation of the cases.

In the late 1980s, the growing evidence of police misconduct and the unreliable nature of the confessions could no longer be ignored. In 1989, the case of the Guildford Four was brought back to the Court of Appeal. The court reviewed the evidence, including the new findings of police fabrication and suppression of evidence that could have exonerated the four. On October 19, 1989, the Court of Appeal quashed the convictions of the Guildford Four, declaring them to be "unsatisfactory and unsafe." The ruling acknowledged the grave injustices that had occurred and the failure of the legal system to protect the rights of the accused.

The release of the Guildford Four was a momentous event, but it did not mark the end of the quest for justice. The case prompted a broader examination of the British legal system and its handling of terrorism-related cases. In the years that followed, several other cases involving alleged IRA members and sympathizers were reviewed, leading to further revelations of wrongful convictions and miscarriages of justice.

The case of the Guildford Four, along with related cases such as the Birmingham Six and the Maguire Seven, highlighted systemic flaws in the criminal justice system, including the use of coerced confessions, inadequate legal representation, and the suppression of exculpatory evidence. These cases underscored the dangers of allowing public and political pressures to influence judicial processes and the importance of safeguarding the rights of the accused, even in the face of national security concerns.

In response to the wrongful convictions, the British government and legal institutions undertook a series of reforms aimed at preventing similar injustices in the future. These reforms included changes to the rules governing police interrogations, the establishment of the Criminal Cases Review Commission (CCRC) to investigate potential miscarriages of justice, and improvements in forensic science standards and practices.

The wrongful convictions also had a profound personal impact on the lives of the individuals involved. Gerry Conlon, in particular, became a prominent advocate for justice reform after his release, writing a memoir titled "Proved Innocent" and working to raise awareness about wrongful convictions and the need for systemic change. Conlon's story, along with those of his fellow wrongly convicted individuals, served as a powerful reminder of the human cost of miscarriages of justice and the importance of vigilance in protecting civil liberties and human rights.

The legacy of the Guildford Four continues to resonate in contemporary discussions about justice and human rights. The case serves as a cautionary tale about the perils of compromising legal principles in the pursuit of security and the necessity of maintaining rigorous standards of fairness and due process in all criminal proceedings. It also underscores the vital role of independent oversight and the need for mechanisms to correct wrongful convictions and hold accountable those responsible for abuses of power.

In popular culture, the story of the Guildford Four has been immortalized in the 1993 film "In the Name of the Father," directed by Jim Sheridan and starring Daniel Day-Lewis as Gerry Conlon. The film dramatizes the events leading up to the wrongful convictions and the eventual exoneration of the Guildford Four, bringing their story to a wider audience and reinforcing the enduring importance of their case in the ongoing struggle for justice and human rights.

The Trial of the Guildford Four remains a stark reminder of the potential for injustice within the legal system, particularly in times of political turmoil and social unrest. It challenges us to uphold the highest standards of fairness and integrity in the administration of justice and to remain vigilant against abuses of power that can lead to wrongful convictions and the denial of fundamental rights. As we reflect on the lessons of the Guildford Four, we are reminded of the critical importance of due process, the presumption of innocence, and the protection of human rights in ensuring a just and equitable society.

95

Chapter 25: The Trial of Sir Thomas More

The trial of Sir Thomas More, an event that encapsulates the complex interplay between law, politics, and personal conscience, stands as a poignant chapter in the history of the English Reformation. Sir Thomas More was a distinguished lawyer, philosopher, author, and statesman, serving as Lord Chancellor under King Henry VIII. His trial and subsequent execution in 1535 were the result of his steadfast opposition to the king's separation from the Catholic Church and the establishment of the Church of England. This trial not only highlights the turbulent period of religious upheaval but also underscores the profound moral and ethical dilemmas faced by individuals during this era.

Thomas More was born in 1478 in London, into a prosperous family. He received an excellent education, attending Oxford University and later studying law at Lincoln's Inn. More's intellectual prowess and deep commitment to his faith earned him a reputation as a leading scholar and a devout Catholic. His most famous work, "Utopia," published in 1516, reflects his humanist ideals and his vision of a society based on reason and justice.

More's rise to prominence in English politics began in earnest in the early 16th century. He entered Parliament in 1504 and quickly became known for his eloquence and integrity. His legal acumen and dedication to public service led to his appointment as Under-Sheriff of London in 1510. More's career continued to flourish, and in 1529, he was appointed Lord Chancellor, the highest judicial position in England, succeeding Cardinal Thomas Wolsey. As Lord Chancellor, More was responsible for overseeing the administration of justice and the management of legal affairs in the kingdom.

More's tenure as Lord Chancellor coincided with a period of significant political and religious turmoil. King Henry VIII, who had initially been a staunch defender of the Catholic Church, sought an annulment of his marriage to Catherine of Aragon. The pope's refusal to grant the annulment prompted Henry to break away from the Roman Catholic Church and establish the Church of England, with himself as its supreme head. This decision was formalized through a series of legislative acts, including the Act of Supremacy in 1534, which declared Henry the Supreme Head of the Church of England, and the Treasons Act, which made it a capital offense to deny the king's supremacy.

Sir Thomas More's deep religious convictions placed him in direct conflict with the king's actions. As a devout Catholic, More could not in good conscience support the annulment or acknowledge Henry as the head of the church. He resigned as Lord Chancellor in 1532, citing ill health and his disapproval of the king's policies. Despite his resignation, More remained a significant figure and a vocal critic of the king's religious reforms. His refusal to attend the coronation of Anne Boleyn, Henry's new queen, further fueled suspicions of his opposition.

In 1534, More was summoned to appear before a commission and swear an oath to the Act of Succession, which declared the offspring of Henry and Anne Boleyn to be legitimate heirs to the throne and required recognition of the king's supremacy over the church. More's refusal to take the oath, based on his religious beliefs, led to his arrest and imprisonment in the Tower of London. During his imprisonment, More was subjected to intense pressure to conform, but he remained resolute in his convictions.

The trial of Sir Thomas More took place on July 1, 1535, at Westminster Hall. The charges against him were based on his refusal to acknowledge the king's supremacy and his alleged conspiracy to undermine the new religious order. The trial was presided over by Sir Thomas Audley, the new Lord Chancellor, and included prominent figures such as Thomas Cromwell, Henry's chief minister, who played a central role in orchestrating the proceedings against More.

The prosecution's case rested heavily on the testimony of Richard Rich, the Solicitor General, who claimed that More had expressed treasonous sentiments during a conversation in the Tower. Rich alleged that More had stated his belief that Parliament had no authority to make the king the head of the church. More vehemently denied the accusation, arguing that his silence on the matter should not be construed as an act of treason. He contended that he had always remained loyal to the king and had never spoken against the Act of Supremacy.

Despite More's eloquent defense, the trial was essentially a foregone conclusion. The jury, likely influenced by the king's desire for a swift conviction, found More guilty of treason. Upon hearing the verdict, More delivered a powerful speech, reaffirming his loyalty to the king but reiterating his commitment to his faith and his refusal to compromise his conscience. He famously declared, "I die the king's good servant, but God's first."

On July 6, 1535, Sir Thomas More was executed by beheading at Tower Hill. His final moments were marked by his unwavering faith and his acceptance of his fate. More's execution sent shockwaves throughout Europe and solidified his legacy as a martyr for the Catholic faith. His steadfastness in the face of persecution and his refusal to compromise his principles made him a symbol of moral integrity and religious conviction.

The trial and execution of Sir Thomas More had profound implications for the English Reformation and the broader political landscape of the time. It demonstrated the extent to which King Henry VIII was willing to go to consolidate his power and enforce his religious reforms. The case also highlighted the dangers of a legal system that could be manipulated for political ends and the risks faced by individuals who dared to oppose the prevailing authority.

In the years following More's execution, his reputation as a martyr and a champion of conscience continued to grow. He was canonized as a saint by the Roman Catholic Church in 1935, and his story has been immortalized in literature, drama, and film. One of the most famous portrayals of More's life is the play "A Man for All Seasons" by Robert Bolt, which was later adapted into an Academy Award-winning film. The play and film capture the moral and ethical dilemmas faced by More and underscore the enduring relevance of his struggle for integrity and justice.

The trial of Sir Thomas More serves as a powerful reminder of the complexities of navigating the intersections of law, politics, and personal belief. It challenges us to consider the importance of conscience and the courage required to stand up for one's principles in the face of overwhelming pressure. More's legacy continues to inspire individuals and societies to uphold the values of justice, integrity, and the inviolability of personal conscience.

In reflecting on the trial of Sir Thomas More, we are reminded of the enduring struggle for religious freedom and the necessity of safeguarding individual rights against the encroachments of political power. More's unwavering commitment to his faith and his refusal to capitulate to the demands of the state serve as a testament to the strength of the human spirit and the profound impact that one individual's courage and conviction can have on the course of history.

Chapter 26: The Trial of Richard Nixon's Aides

The Trial of Richard Nixon's aides, known as the Watergate trials, stands as a critical juncture in American legal and political history. The Watergate scandal, which ultimately led to the resignation of President Nixon, began with the break-in at the Democratic National Committee headquarters at the Watergate office complex in Washington, D.C., on June 17, 1972. This seemingly minor incident set off a chain reaction that exposed deep-seated corruption and abuse of power at the highest levels of government. The trials of Nixon's aides were the legal culmination of this scandal and involved some of the most powerful figures in American politics, bringing to light the extent of illegal activities sanctioned by the Nixon administration.

The break-in was carried out by five men who were soon linked to the Committee to Re-Elect the President (CREEP), a fundraising organization for Nixon's re-election campaign. The initial investigation did not immediately implicate Nixon or his close aides, but the story gradually unfolded, revealing a complex web of espionage, sabotage, and cover-up. Two key journalists from The Washington Post, Bob Woodward and Carl Bernstein, played a crucial role in uncovering the truth, aided by their secret informant, known as "Deep Throat," later revealed to be FBI Associate Director Mark Felt. Their persistent reporting kept the story alive and drew public and congressional attention to the scandal.

As the investigation deepened, it became clear that high-ranking officials within the Nixon administration were involved. The subsequent trials and Senate hearings revealed that the break-in was part of a larger campaign of political espionage and sabotage conducted on behalf of the Nixon re-election effort. The most significant aspect of the Watergate scandal was not the break-in itself but the cover-up that followed, orchestrated by Nixon and his aides. This cover-up involved paying hush money to the burglars, using the CIA to obstruct the FBI's investigation, and destroying evidence.

The legal proceedings began in earnest with the trial of the Watergate burglars in early 1973. The five burglars, along with two others implicated in the break-in, were tried before Judge John Sirica. The trial revealed that the burglars had been paid for their silence, and under intense questioning from Judge Sirica, they began to implicate higher-ups in the Nixon administration. The most significant development came when one of the burglars, James McCord, wrote a letter to Sirica stating that there had been political pressure to plead guilty and remain silent. This letter blew the cover off the Watergate scandal, indicating that the conspiracy extended into the White House.

Following this revelation, a series of high-profile indictments and trials ensued, targeting Nixon's closest aides. Among those indicted were H.R. Haldeman, Nixon's Chief of Staff; John Ehrlichman, Assistant to the President for Domestic Affairs; John N. Mitchell, former Attorney General and head of CREEP; and Charles Colson, Special Counsel to the President. These individuals, along with others, were charged with various crimes, including conspiracy, obstruction of justice, and perjury.

The Senate established the Senate Watergate Committee, chaired by Senator Sam Ervin, to investigate the scandal. The committee's televised hearings in 1973 captivated the nation and revealed the extent of the Nixon administration's involvement in illegal activities. Testimonies from key witnesses, such as John Dean, White House Counsel, who turned state's witness, provided damning evidence of the cover-up. Dean's testimony implicated Nixon directly, stating that the president had been involved in discussions about the cover-up as early as March 1973.

One of the most significant pieces of evidence uncovered during the hearings was the existence of the White House tapes. Alexander

Butterfield, a former presidential aide, revealed that Nixon had a secret taping system in the Oval Office, which recorded all conversations. The tapes became the focal point of the investigation, as they were believed to contain concrete evidence of Nixon's involvement in the cover-up. Nixon initially refused to release the tapes, citing executive privilege, but the Supreme Court, in United States v. Nixon, ruled unanimously that the president had to turn them over to the special prosecutor.

The tapes indeed provided smoking-gun evidence of Nixon's complicity in the cover-up, leading to a dramatic shift in the political landscape. Facing imminent impeachment, Nixon resigned on August 8, 1974, becoming the first president in American history to do so. His resignation did not halt the legal proceedings against his aides, who continued to face trial and sentencing.

Haldeman, Ehrlichman, and Mitchell were convicted of conspiracy, obstruction of justice, and perjury in January 1975. Haldeman and Ehrlichman were sentenced to 18 months to 8 years in prison, while Mitchell received a sentence of 2 1/2 to 8 years. Charles Colson, who had pleaded guilty to obstruction of justice, served seven months in prison. These convictions underscored the severity of the crimes committed and the far-reaching implications of the Watergate scandal.

The trials of Nixon's aides were not just a legal reckoning but a profound moment of accountability in American history. They demonstrated the resilience of the legal and political systems in holding powerful figures accountable, even at the highest levels of government. The Watergate scandal and the subsequent trials had a lasting impact on American politics and governance, leading to greater transparency and reforms designed to prevent such abuses of power in the future. The scandal also eroded public trust in government, a sentiment that has had enduring consequences for American political culture.

Chapter 27: The Trial of Saddam Hussein

The trial of Saddam Hussein, one of the most notorious and significant legal proceedings in modern history, unfolded as a dramatic and complex event that sought to bring to justice the former dictator of Iraq. Following his capture in December 2003 by American forces, Saddam Hussein faced a series of charges related to crimes against humanity, war crimes, and genocide committed during his brutal regime, which lasted from 1979 until his overthrow in 2003. The trial not only aimed to hold Saddam accountable for his actions but also to provide a sense of closure and justice for the countless victims of his reign.

The legal process began with the establishment of the Iraqi Special Tribunal (IST) in December 2003, created specifically to prosecute members of Saddam's regime for atrocities committed during their rule. The tribunal faced numerous challenges from the outset, including questions about its legitimacy, security concerns, and the sheer scale of the crimes committed. Despite these obstacles, the IST was determined to proceed, reflecting the Iraqi government's and the international community's resolve to bring Saddam to justice.

Saddam Hussein's trial officially commenced on October 19, 2005, in Baghdad, with Saddam and seven co-defendants facing charges related to the 1982 massacre of 148 Shiite men and boys in the town of Dujail. This incident was selected as the initial case due to the availability of evidence and the relatively straightforward nature of the charges. The massacre occurred in retaliation for an assassination attempt on Saddam's life during a visit to Dujail, resulting in widespread arrests, torture, and executions ordered by Saddam and carried out by his security forces.

The trial quickly became a focal point for international attention, with media outlets around the world closely monitoring the proceedings. The courtroom was tense, with Saddam frequently challenging the tribunal's authority and attempting to use the trial as a platform to defend his regime and condemn the U.S.-led invasion of Iraq. Saddam's defiant behavior, including shouting at judges and refusing to recognize the court's legitimacy, underscored the trial's contentious nature.

One of the significant aspects of the trial was the presentation of evidence and testimonies from survivors, witnesses, and former officials. The prosecution detailed the systematic torture and execution of detainees, presenting documents and personal accounts that painted a harrowing picture of the regime's brutality. Witnesses recounted their experiences of arrest, torture, and the loss of family members, providing poignant and powerful testimony that underscored the human cost of Saddam's rule.

The defense, led by a team of Iraqi and international lawyers, argued that Saddam was acting within his legal rights as the head of state and that the actions taken in Dujail were necessary measures to maintain national security. The defense also questioned the legitimacy of the tribunal, arguing that it was an instrument of the occupying forces and lacked impartiality. Despite these arguments, the overwhelming evidence presented by the prosecution made it clear that the Dujail massacre was part of a broader pattern of systematic repression and violence perpetrated by Saddam's regime.

Throughout the trial, security concerns were a constant issue. Judges, lawyers, and witnesses faced significant threats, with several defense attorneys being assassinated during the proceedings. The tribunal operated under tight security, with sessions often delayed or disrupted due to security incidents. These challenges highlighted the volatile and dangerous environment in which the trial was conducted, reflecting the ongoing instability in post-invasion Iraq.

On November 5, 2006, the tribunal reached a verdict. Saddam Hussein was found guilty of crimes against humanity for his role in the Dujail massacre and sentenced to death by hanging. The verdict was met with mixed reactions; while many Iraqis and international observers saw it as a necessary step toward justice and accountability, others viewed it as a politically motivated act by the Iraqi government and its allies.

Saddam's defense team immediately announced plans to appeal the verdict, but the appeals process was swift. On December 26, 2006, the Iraqi appellate court upheld the death sentence, paving the way for Saddam's execution. Despite international calls for a fairer and more transparent process, the Iraqi government proceeded with the execution, which took place on December 30, 2006.

Saddam Hussein's execution was a highly symbolic and controversial event. For many Iraqis, it marked the end of a dark chapter in their history and a form of retribution for the suffering endured under his regime. However, the manner in which the execution was carried out, including the circulation of graphic footage showing Saddam being taunted by guards before his death, drew widespread criticism and highlighted the deep sectarian divisions within Iraq.

The trial of Saddam Hussein was not the end of legal proceedings related to his regime. Other high-ranking officials, including his half-brother Barzan Ibrahim al-Tikriti and former Vice President Taha Yassin Ramadan, also faced trials and were subsequently convicted and executed for their roles in the Dujail massacre and other crimes. Additionally, the IST continued to investigate and prosecute cases related to other atrocities committed by the regime, such as the Anfal campaign against the Kurds, the suppression of the 1991 uprisings, and the forced displacement of the Marsh Arabs.

The broader impact of Saddam Hussein's trial and execution extends beyond the immediate legal and political ramifications. The trial was a significant moment for international justice, demonstrating the possibility of holding even the most powerful and repressive leaders accountable for their actions. It also highlighted the challenges and complexities of conducting trials in post-conflict settings, where security concerns, political pressures, and questions of legitimacy can complicate the pursuit of justice.

However, the trial also underscored the limitations and criticisms of the Iraqi Special Tribunal. Critics argued that the tribunal lacked the necessary impartiality and procedural rigor to deliver a truly fair trial, pointing to the rushed nature of the proceedings, the influence of the occupying forces, and the challenges faced by the defense team. These concerns have led to ongoing debates about the effectiveness and fairness of the IST and its legacy in the broader context of transitional justice.

The trial of Saddam Hussein remains a defining moment in Iraq's history and a crucial case study for international law and justice. It exemplifies the potential for accountability and the rule of law to address the crimes of repressive regimes, while also highlighting the inherent challenges and controversies involved in such processes. The trial's impact continues to be felt in Iraq and beyond, serving as both a cautionary tale and a testament to the enduring quest for justice in the face of tyranny.

Chapter 28: The Trial of the Scottsboro Boys

The trial of the Scottsboro Boys stands as one of the most significant and controversial legal battles in American history, embodying the racial tensions, injustices, and flaws of the U.S. legal system during the 1930s. The case involved nine African American teenagers falsely accused of raping two white women aboard a train in Alabama in 1931. The ensuing trials and retrials, marked by a pervasive climate of racial prejudice and legal impropriety, spanned nearly two decades and highlighted the systemic racism and urgent need for legal reforms in the United States.

The incident that led to the trial began on March 25, 1931, when nine black youths—Charlie Weems, Clarence Norris, Andy Wright, Roy Wright, Olen Montgomery, Eugene Williams, Ozie Powell, Willie Roberson, and Haywood Patterson—were pulled from a freight train in Paint Rock, Alabama, following an altercation with white hobos. After the altercation, the train was stopped by an armed posse in Scottsboro, Alabama, and the nine boys were arrested. Two white women, Victoria Price and Ruby Bates, who had also been riding the train illegally, accused the boys of raping them. These accusations led to immediate outrage and calls for swift justice, reflective of the deeply entrenched racial biases of the time.

The first set of trials took place in Scottsboro in April 1931, a mere two weeks after the arrests. The atmosphere in the courtroom was charged with hostility, as angry mobs gathered outside, demanding the boys' execution. The defendants were represented by inexperienced and underprepared court-appointed attorneys, who failed to adequately defend them. Despite the lack of substantial evidence and the dubious credibility of the accusers, all nine boys were swiftly convicted by all-white juries. Eight of the boys were sentenced to death, while the youngest, Roy Wright, was given a life sentence due to his age.

The initial verdicts drew national and international attention, prompting outrage and mobilizing support from various organizations and individuals. The International Labor Defense (ILD), an affiliate of the Communist Party USA, took up the cause, providing legal representation and publicizing the case to garner support. The involvement of the ILD added a layer of political complexity, as it sought to highlight the case as a symbol of broader social and racial injustice in America.

The first major breakthrough came in 1932 when the U.S. Supreme Court agreed to review the case. In Powell v. Alabama, the Court overturned the convictions, ruling that the defendants had been denied effective legal counsel, a violation of their Fourteenth Amendment rights. This landmark decision emphasized the necessity of adequate legal representation, particularly in capital cases, and set a precedent for future cases involving the right to counsel.

Despite this victory, the struggle for justice was far from over. The boys faced numerous retrials, each marked by the same prejudicial attitudes and flawed legal procedures. The second round of trials, held in Decatur, Alabama, in 1933, saw renowned defense attorney Samuel Leibowitz take the lead in defending the boys. Leibowitz, a Jewish lawyer from New York, faced intense hostility and threats from the local community, reflecting the deep-seated anti-Semitism and racism of the period.

During these retrials, Ruby Bates recanted her testimony, admitting that she and Victoria Price had fabricated the rape allegations to avoid arrest for vagrancy and to deflect attention from their own illicit activities. Despite this, the juries remained largely unmoved by the new evidence, and the boys were again convicted. Leibowitz's passionate defense and the mounting evidence of innocence highlighted the blatant racial injustice at play, but they struggled to overcome the entrenched biases of the Southern legal system.

In 1935, the U.S. Supreme Court once again intervened in the case with Norris v. Alabama, ruling that the systematic exclusion of African Americans from jury service denied the defendants a fair trial. This decision was another significant step forward, addressing the pervasive issue of racial discrimination in jury selection. However, it did not immediately lead to the boys' exoneration.

The legal battles continued through the late 1930s, with various convictions being overturned, retrials ordered, and some charges eventually dropped. Haywood Patterson and Clarence Norris became particularly notable figures, enduring multiple trials and convictions. Patterson managed to escape from prison in 1948, but his life continued to be marred by the stigma of the false accusations. Norris, who was paroled in 1946, spent much of his later life seeking a full pardon.

The Scottsboro case had far-reaching implications beyond the courtroom. It galvanized the civil rights movement, drawing attention to the systemic racism and injustices faced by African Americans in the South. It also spurred significant legal reforms, including the establishment of fairer trial procedures and the inclusion of African Americans in jury pools. The case underscored the importance of vigilant defense against racial prejudice in the legal system and highlighted the critical role of legal representation in ensuring justice.

Public opinion on the Scottsboro case was deeply divided, reflecting the broader societal tensions of the era. In the North, the case was widely seen as a miscarriage of justice, sparking protests, fundraising campaigns, and advocacy efforts. Prominent figures such as Langston Hughes, W.E.B. Du Bois, and Eleanor Roosevelt voiced their support for the Scottsboro Boys, using their platforms to draw attention to the case. Conversely, in the South, the prevailing sentiment remained largely hostile, with many viewing the boys as guilty despite the mounting evidence of their innocence.

The legacy of the Scottsboro case continued to resonate in the decades following the trials. It served as a catalyst for subsequent civil rights efforts, inspiring activists and lawyers to challenge racial discrimination in the legal system. The case also influenced popular culture, with numerous books, plays, and films drawing on its themes and highlighting its significance.

In the 1970s and 1980s, efforts to achieve posthumous justice for the Scottsboro Boys gained momentum. Clarence Norris, the last surviving defendant, received a full pardon from Alabama Governor George Wallace in 1976, acknowledging the wrongful convictions and the immense suffering endured by the boys. In 2013, more than 80 years after the initial trials, the Alabama Board of Pardons and Paroles issued posthumous pardons for the remaining Scottsboro Boys, formally recognizing their innocence and the grave injustices they had faced.

The trial of the Scottsboro Boys remains a powerful reminder of the enduring impact of racial prejudice on the legal system and the importance of continuing efforts to ensure fairness and justice for all. It highlights the need for vigilance in defending the rights of the accused, particularly in cases where racial bias may influence proceedings. The case also underscores the critical role of public advocacy and legal intervention in challenging systemic injustices and fostering a more equitable society.

Chapter 29: The Trial of Chelsea Manning

The trial of Chelsea Manning, a U.S. Army intelligence analyst, became a landmark case in the history of whistleblowing, government transparency, and the handling of classified information. Born Bradley Manning, Chelsea Manning's trial and subsequent conviction for leaking classified documents to WikiLeaks in 2010 exposed deep-seated issues within the U.S. military and government. Manning's actions and the resulting legal battle ignited intense debates over national security, transparency, and the ethical responsibilities of those in positions of power.

Chelsea Manning's journey to becoming a whistleblower began during her deployment to Iraq in 2009. As an intelligence analyst, she had access to vast amounts of classified information. Manning became increasingly disillusioned with the U.S. military's operations and policies, particularly the apparent disregard for human life and the lack of transparency in reporting incidents involving civilian casualties and other sensitive issues. This growing sense of moral and ethical conflict led Manning to believe that the public had a right to know about the information she was privy to.

In early 2010, Manning made the fateful decision to leak a trove of classified documents to WikiLeaks, an international non-profit organization known for publishing secret information, news leaks, and classified media provided by anonymous sources. The leaked materials included diplomatic cables, military incident logs from the wars in Iraq and Afghanistan, and a classified video showing a 2007 Apache helicopter attack in Baghdad that killed multiple people, including two Reuters journalists. Dubbed the "Collateral Murder" video, this footage garnered significant attention and sparked outrage worldwide.

The release of these documents had profound implications. On one hand, supporters of Manning hailed her as a courageous whistleblower who exposed government misconduct and the human cost of war. On the other hand, critics condemned her actions as a reckless betrayal of her duty, arguing that the leaks jeopardized national security, endangered lives, and strained diplomatic relations.

Manning was arrested in May 2010 after Adrian Lamo, a former hacker with whom she had been corresponding online, reported her to the authorities. Manning was charged with 22 offenses under the Uniform Code of Military Justice (UCMJ), including violations of the Espionage Act, theft of government property, and "aiding the enemy," a charge that carried the potential for a death sentence. The trial proceedings began in 2012, with Manning held in pretrial detention under conditions that drew international criticism for being excessively harsh and inhumane.

The court-martial of Chelsea Manning commenced in June 2013 at Fort Meade, Maryland. The prosecution's case focused on the argument that Manning had knowingly endangered national security and put lives at risk by leaking the classified documents. They contended that Manning's actions amounted to "aiding the enemy" by making sensitive information available to adversaries of the United States, including terrorist organizations like al-Qaeda. To bolster their case, the prosecution presented expert witnesses who testified about the potential harm caused by the leaks and the significance of the compromised information.

Manning's defense team, led by civilian attorney David Coombs, argued that Manning's motivations were rooted in a desire to expose wrongdoing and spark public debate about U.S. military and foreign policy. They emphasized that Manning had not intended to harm the United States or its interests but rather sought to promote transparency and accountability. The defense also highlighted Manning's struggles with gender identity, arguing that her personal distress and isolation contributed to her decision to leak the documents.

Throughout the trial, Manning took the stand and admitted to leaking the documents, expressing remorse for the unintended consequences of her actions but maintaining that she believed she was doing the right thing at the time. She also detailed the harsh conditions of her pretrial confinement, which included extended periods of solitary confinement and other punitive measures that drew condemnation from human rights organizations.

In July 2013, Manning was acquitted of the most serious charge of "aiding the enemy" but found guilty of 17 of the 22 charges, including multiple counts under the Espionage Act and theft of government property. The following month, she was sentenced to 35 years in prison, a sentence that was widely criticized as being excessively harsh given the non-violent nature of her offenses and the significant public interest served by the disclosures.

The trial and subsequent imprisonment of Chelsea Manning had far-reaching implications for the broader discourse on whistleblowing, government transparency, and the protection of classified information. Her case became a rallying point for activists, journalists, and civil liberties organizations who argued that the U.S. government's response to her leaks was emblematic of an overzealous and punitive approach to whistleblowers. They contended that Manning's actions had exposed critical issues related to military conduct, human rights abuses, and the limits of governmental transparency.

Manning's case also intersected with broader debates about the treatment of individuals in the LGBTQ+ community within the military and the criminal justice system. In 2013, shortly after her sentencing, Manning publicly announced her gender transition and intention to live as a woman, adopting the name Chelsea. Her request for hormone therapy and other medical treatments while incarcerated highlighted the challenges faced by transgender individuals in prison and sparked further debate about the rights and treatment of LGBTQ+ prisoners.

In 2017, after serving seven years in prison, Chelsea Manning's sentence was commuted by President Barack Obama in one of his final acts in office. Obama's decision was met with mixed reactions; supporters viewed it as a recognition of the excessive nature of Manning's sentence and the value of her disclosures, while critics argued that it set a dangerous precedent by appearing to condone the unauthorized release of classified information.

Manning's release did not mark the end of her involvement in public and political discourse. She continued to advocate for transparency, government accountability, and the rights of transgender individuals, often speaking out on issues related to whistleblowing and civil liberties. Her case remains a touchstone in discussions about the balance between national security and the public's right to know, as well as the treatment of whistleblowers within the legal system.

The legacy of Chelsea Manning's trial is multifaceted. It underscores the profound impact that individual acts of whistleblowing can have on public awareness and policy debates, while also highlighting the severe consequences faced by those who choose to leak classified information. The case serves as a stark reminder of the tensions between governmental authority and individual conscience, illustrating the challenges of navigating the ethical and legal complexities inherent in the disclosure of sensitive information.

In the years following Manning's trial, the landscape of whistleblowing and government transparency continued to evolve. Cases such as those involving Edward Snowden and Julian Assange further fueled debates about the appropriate limits of secrecy and the protections afforded to whistleblowers. These cases, alongside Manning's, contributed to ongoing discussions about the need for legal reforms to better balance national security interests with the public's right to information and the protection of whistleblowers.

Ultimately, the trial of Chelsea Manning stands as a pivotal moment in the ongoing struggle to define the boundaries of transparency, accountability, and ethical responsibility within the context of national security. It challenges society to reflect on the values of openness and justice, and to consider how best to protect those who risk their freedom to expose truths that they believe the public has a right to know.

Chapter 30: The Trial of Aung San Suu Kyi

The trial of Aung San Suu Kyi, a Nobel Peace Prize laureate and the de facto leader of Myanmar, stands as a defining moment in the nation's tumultuous journey toward democracy and reflects the ongoing struggle between military authority and civilian governance. Aung San Suu Kyi's life has been marked by her steadfast commitment to democracy and human rights, and her trials are emblematic of the broader political and social conflicts within Myanmar.

Aung San Suu Kyi, born in 1945, is the daughter of Aung San, a revered hero of Myanmar's independence movement. Her early life was influenced by her father's legacy and her education in India and the United Kingdom, where she developed a deep understanding of democratic principles and governance. She returned to Myanmar in 1988, during a period of significant political upheaval, and quickly became the face of the pro-democracy movement against the ruling military junta.

The 1988 uprising, which saw massive protests against the military regime, was brutally suppressed, leading to thousands of deaths and the imprisonment of many activists. Aung San Suu Kyi emerged as a prominent leader of the National League for Democracy (NLD), advocating for peaceful resistance and democratic reforms. Her speeches and writings, emphasizing nonviolence and the power of the people, resonated with millions of Myanmar citizens yearning for change.

In 1990, the military government called for a general election, which the NLD won by a landslide, securing 81% of the parliamentary seats. However, the junta refused to recognize the results and placed Aung San Suu Kyi under house arrest, where she would spend much of the next two decades. Despite international pressure and calls for her release, the military maintained its grip on power, citing various justifications to extend her detention.

Aung San Suu Kyi's house arrest garnered global attention, and she became an international symbol of peaceful resistance and the struggle for democracy. She was awarded the Nobel Peace Prize in 1991 while still under detention. Her continued imprisonment drew widespread condemnation from governments, human rights organizations, and individuals around the world, who saw her detention as a blatant violation of human rights and democratic principles.

Her release in 2010 marked a significant turning point, coinciding with a period of tentative political reforms by the military junta. These reforms led to a semi-civilian government, and in 2012, Aung San Suu Kyi was elected to parliament in a by-election. The NLD won a resounding victory in the 2015 general election, and while Aung San Suu Kyi was constitutionally barred from becoming president, she assumed the role of State Counsellor, effectively serving as the country's leader.

However, her time in office was marred by significant challenges, including ethnic conflicts and the Rohingya crisis. The military's crackdown on the Rohingya Muslim minority in 2017, which the United Nations described as a "textbook example of ethnic cleansing," severely tarnished her international reputation. While Aung San Suu Kyi defended the military's actions at the International Court of Justice, her stance was criticized for seemingly ignoring human rights abuses and undermining her legacy as a human rights champion.

The tenuous relationship between the NLD-led civilian government and the military culminated in the coup of February 1, 2021, which abruptly ended Myanmar's brief experiment with quasi-democracy. The military, citing unsubstantiated claims of electoral fraud in the 2020 general election (which the NLD won by an even larger margin than in 2015), detained Aung San Suu Kyi and other NLD leaders, sparking widespread protests and international condemnation.

Following the coup, Aung San Suu Kyi faced a series of criminal charges brought by the military junta, including allegations of corruption, violation of COVID-19 regulations, illegal importation and possession of walkie-talkies, and breaching the Official Secrets Act. The charges were widely seen as politically motivated, aimed at discrediting and silencing her, and preventing her from returning to political life.

The trial proceedings were held in a closed court, with limited access for her lawyers and the media, leading to concerns about the fairness and transparency of the judicial process. The conditions of her detention and the handling of the trial drew criticism from human rights organizations and foreign governments, who called for her immediate release and a return to democratic governance in Myanmar.

In December 2021, Aung San Suu Kyi was found guilty of incitement and violating COVID-19 restrictions and sentenced to four years in prison, a sentence that was later reduced to two years. This conviction was the first of several verdicts in ongoing trials against her, reflecting the military's determination to eliminate her influence and consolidate its power. Subsequent trials resulted in additional convictions and extended her prison sentence.

The broader implications of Aung San Suu Kyi's trial are profound, both for Myanmar and the international community. Domestically, her imprisonment symbolizes the ongoing struggle between democratic aspirations and authoritarian rule in Myanmar. The military's actions have provoked widespread civil disobedience and resistance, with pro-democracy activists, ethnic groups, and ordinary citizens uniting in opposition to the junta. The brutal suppression of protests and the intensification of armed conflict have plunged the country into turmoil, exacerbating humanitarian crises and destabilizing the region.

Internationally, Aung San Suu Kyi's trial has highlighted the challenges of promoting democracy and human rights in an environment where authoritarian regimes wield significant power. The response from the global community has included sanctions against military leaders, calls for an arms embargo, and efforts to support the pro-democracy movement in Myanmar. However, the geopolitical complexities of the region and the military's entrenched position have made it difficult to achieve meaningful change.

Aung San Suu Kyi's legacy is complex and multifaceted. While her earlier years of house arrest and advocacy for democracy earned her widespread admiration, her later years in power and her response to the Rohingya crisis have drawn significant criticism. Nevertheless, her enduring influence and the symbolic power of her struggle continue to inspire many in Myanmar and around the world.

The trial of Aung San Suu Kyi is not just a legal battle but a reflection of the broader fight for the soul of Myanmar. It underscores the fragility of democratic institutions in the face of authoritarianism and the enduring power of individual resistance against oppressive regimes. As Myanmar navigates its uncertain future, the fate of Aung San Suu Kyi remains a pivotal element in the broader narrative of the country's quest for democracy and justice. Her trial, and the ongoing struggle of the Myanmar people, serves as a poignant reminder of the enduring challenges and the resilience required to achieve true freedom and democracy.

Chapter 31: The Trial of Leo Frank

The trial of Leo Frank is one of the most notorious and controversial legal cases in American history, encapsulating themes of anti-Semitism, racial tension, and injustice in the early 20th century. Leo Frank was a Jewish factory manager in Atlanta, Georgia, who was accused and convicted of the murder of a 13-year-old girl named Mary Phagan in 1913. The trial and its aftermath not only exposed the deep-seated prejudices of the time but also led to significant legal and social repercussions.

Mary Phagan worked at the National Pencil Company in Atlanta, where Leo Frank was the superintendent. On April 26, 1913, Phagan came to the factory to collect her pay and was later found dead in the building's basement. Her body showed signs of blunt force trauma and strangulation, and she had been sexually assaulted. The brutality of the crime shocked the community and led to an intense public outcry.

The initial investigation focused on several suspects, including Newt Lee, the factory's African American night watchman, and Jim Conley, an African American janitor at the factory. However, suspicion quickly fell on Leo Frank, who had been one of the last people to see Phagan alive. Frank's status as a Northerner and a Jew in the predominantly Christian South made him an easy target for public anger and prejudice.

Frank was arrested and charged with the murder of Mary Phagan. The trial began on July 28, 1913, and was held in the Fulton County Courthouse in Atlanta. The prosecution, led by Hugh Dorsey, presented a case based largely on circumstantial evidence and the testimony of Jim Conley. Conley claimed that he had helped Frank dispose of Phagan's body after Frank had killed her. Conley's testimony was crucial, as he provided a detailed account of the crime that implicated Frank as the murderer.

The defense, led by attorneys Luther Rosser and Reuben Arnold, argued that Frank was innocent and that Conley was the true culprit. They pointed out numerous inconsistencies in Conley's testimony and highlighted his criminal background. The defense also presented witnesses who testified to Frank's good character and attempted to establish an alibi for him. Despite these efforts, the public mood was heavily against Frank, fueled by sensationalist media coverage and widespread anti-Semitic sentiments.

The trial was marked by a highly charged atmosphere, with crowds gathering outside the courthouse and public opinion overwhelmingly against Frank. The jury, influenced by the intense public pressure and the prevailing prejudices, found Frank guilty of murder on August 25, 1913. He was sentenced to death by hanging, a verdict that was met with cheers and celebration from the gathered crowds.

Following the conviction, Frank's legal team launched a series of appeals, arguing that the trial had been unfair and that new evidence had emerged that could exonerate him. These appeals were denied by the Georgia Supreme Court, and the case reached the U.S. Supreme Court, which also declined to overturn the conviction. However, the legal battle brought national attention to the case, with many prominent figures and organizations, including the American Jewish community and the newly formed Anti-Defamation League, advocating for Frank's innocence.

In 1915, Georgia Governor John M. Slaton, after reviewing the case and considering the doubts raised about Frank's guilt, commuted Frank's sentence from death to life imprisonment. This decision was deeply unpopular in Georgia and led to public outrage. Mobs protested outside the governor's mansion, and Slaton was forced to leave the state for his own safety.

The commutation did not end the violence against Frank. On August 17, 1915, a group of men, later known as the "Knights of Mary Phagan," broke into the state prison farm where Frank was being held.

They kidnapped Frank and took him to Marietta, Georgia, where they lynched him. Frank's body was hanged from a tree, and the lynching was witnessed by a crowd that included many prominent members of the community.

The lynching of Leo Frank was a horrific act of mob justice and highlighted the pervasive anti-Semitism and racism in the South. It had significant consequences for American society and the legal system. The case spurred the growth of the Anti-Defamation League, which was founded in response to the anti-Semitic fervor surrounding the trial. The ADL became a prominent civil rights organization, dedicated to fighting anti-Semitism and all forms of bigotry.

The trial and lynching of Leo Frank also had a profound impact on the Jewish community in the United States. It underscored the vulnerability of Jews in America and the extent of anti-Semitic prejudice. The case became a rallying point for Jewish Americans, galvanizing efforts to combat discrimination and promote civil rights.

In addition to its social impact, the Leo Frank case prompted changes in the legal system. It highlighted the need for greater protections for defendants and the importance of ensuring fair trials, free from the influence of public opinion and prejudice. The case also underscored the dangers of relying on circumstantial evidence and the testimony of questionable witnesses.

Decades later, in 1986, the Georgia State Board of Pardons and Paroles posthumously pardoned Leo Frank, acknowledging the state's failure to protect him and the unfairness of the trial. The pardon, however, did not exonerate Frank of the crime, but it was a symbolic gesture recognizing the injustice he had suffered.

The Leo Frank case remains a poignant reminder of the dangers of prejudice and the importance of upholding the principles of justice and fairness. It serves as a historical example of the profound impact that bias and discrimination can have on the legal system and the lives of individuals. The trial and its aftermath continue to be studied and remembered as a cautionary tale of injustice and the enduring struggle for civil rights in America.

Chapter 32: The Trial of John Peter Zenger

The trial of John Peter Zenger in 1735 is a landmark case in American history that laid the groundwork for the freedom of the press and highlighted the importance of the right to free speech. This case is often celebrated as a pivotal moment in the development of American legal and constitutional principles, particularly those concerning the rights of individuals to criticize their government and to be protected from libel charges when doing so.

John Peter Zenger was a German immigrant who arrived in New York in 1710. He became a printer and, in 1733, began publishing the New York Weekly Journal. This newspaper quickly became known for its critical stance against the colonial governor of New York, William Cosby. At that time, the governor's administration was embroiled in several controversies, including disputes over land grants, judicial appointments, and alleged corruption. Zenger's newspaper published a series of articles and editorials that harshly criticized Cosby's administration, accusing it of corruption, incompetence, and tyranny.

The New York Weekly Journal was not authored by Zenger alone; it featured contributions from a group of prominent local lawyers and politicians, including James Alexander and William Smith, who were opposed to Governor Cosby's policies. These articles were often anonymous or written under pseudonyms, but their incendiary content made Zenger the target of the governor's wrath. Cosby sought to suppress the newspaper and silence its critics by using his authority to initiate a legal action against Zenger.

On November 17, 1734, Zenger was arrested and charged with seditious libel, a serious offense at the time, which involved the publication of statements intended to incite rebellion against the government. Zenger was imprisoned for more than eight months before his trial, during which time his newspaper continued to publish with his wife, Anna Zenger, taking over the operations. This period in jail was marked by poor conditions, but Zenger remained steadfast in his resolve to fight the charges against him.

The trial began on August 4, 1735, in the courtroom of the Supreme Court of Judicature of the Province of New York. The presiding judge was Chief Justice James Delancey, who was appointed by Governor Cosby and was known for his loyalty to the governor. The prosecution was led by Richard Bradley, the Attorney General of the colony, who argued that Zenger's publications were false, scandalous, and malicious, and that they were designed to undermine the authority of the government.

Zenger's initial defense attorneys, James Alexander and William Smith, were disbarred early in the proceedings after challenging the legality of the judge's commission. This action left Zenger without legal representation until Andrew Hamilton, a respected lawyer from Philadelphia, agreed to defend him. Hamilton's involvement was significant, as he was widely regarded as one of the best attorneys in the colonies, and his defense strategy would ultimately become a defining moment in the trial.

Hamilton's defense was revolutionary for its time. Instead of arguing that Zenger had not published the articles in question, Hamilton admitted that Zenger had printed them but asserted that the articles were not libelous if they were true. This was a bold move, as the prevailing legal doctrine of the time did not consider the truth of a statement to be a defense against libel. According to the law, any published statement that brought the government into disrepute was considered libelous, regardless of its veracity.

In his arguments, Hamilton emphasized the importance of a free press and the right of the people to criticize their government. He contended that if the statements Zenger published were true, then they were not libelous, because the public had a right to know the truth about their leaders. Hamilton argued that the prosecution had failed to prove that the statements were false and that the jury should be the judges of both the law and the facts in the case.

Hamilton's closing argument is particularly memorable for its eloquence and its passionate defense of free speech. He implored the jury to consider the broader implications of their verdict, stating that the case was not just about Zenger but about the liberty of every American. He argued that a free press was essential to the functioning of a free society and that without the ability to criticize their leaders, the people would be at the mercy of tyrants.

The jury, influenced by Hamilton's powerful arguments, returned a verdict of not guilty after only a brief deliberation. This decision was a stunning defeat for the governor and a resounding victory for Zenger and his supporters. The acquittal was widely celebrated as a triumph for freedom of the press and set a precedent that would influence American legal thought for generations to come.

The trial of John Peter Zenger had several significant and lasting impacts on American society and legal practice. Firstly, it established the principle that the truth of a statement can be a defense against charges of libel. This was a major departure from the English common law tradition and laid the foundation for the development of American libel law.

Secondly, the trial underscored the importance of a free and independent press as a check on governmental power. It highlighted the role of the press in holding public officials accountable and in informing the public about matters of public concern. This principle would later be enshrined in the First Amendment to the United States Constitution, which guarantees freedom of the press.

Thirdly, the Zenger trial demonstrated the power of jury nullification, where a jury refuses to convict a defendant despite the evidence against them because they believe the law itself is unjust. In this case, the jury's refusal to convict Zenger was a clear rejection of the existing libel laws and an assertion of their belief in the importance of free expression.

The trial also had a profound impact on the career and legacy of Andrew Hamilton, who was celebrated as a hero for his defense of Zenger. Hamilton's arguments and his success in the case solidified his reputation as a champion of civil liberties and an advocate for the rights of individuals against the power of the state.

In the years following the trial, the case of John Peter Zenger continued to be cited and referenced in legal arguments and writings about press freedom and libel law. It became a foundational story in the narrative of American liberty and the struggle for democratic principles. The trial's legacy can be seen in the robust protections for freedom of the press that exist in the United States today, as well as in the broader cultural value placed on the right to free speech and the importance of holding government accountable.

Chapter 33: The Trial of Timothy McVeigh

The trial of Timothy McVeigh, who was convicted for the 1995 Oklahoma City bombing, stands as one of the most significant and high-profile legal proceedings in the United States in the latter half of the 20th century. This tragic event, which resulted in the deaths of 168 people and injured over 600, remains the deadliest act of domestic terrorism in American history. The trial not only sought justice for the victims but also delved deep into the mind and motivations of a domestic terrorist, examining the broader implications for national security, law enforcement, and the judicial system.

On April 19, 1995, a massive explosion rocked the Alfred P. Murrah Federal Building in downtown Oklahoma City. The blast, caused by a truck bomb, obliterated the front of the nine-story building and caused extensive damage to nearby structures. The immediate aftermath was chaotic and devastating, with rescue workers frantically searching for survivors amidst the rubble. The attack claimed the lives of 168 people, including 19 children who were in the building's daycare center. This horrific act of violence shocked the nation and triggered one of the largest criminal investigations in U.S. history.

In the wake of the bombing, law enforcement agencies, including the FBI and ATF, mobilized rapidly. Within 90 minutes of the explosion, Timothy McVeigh was arrested by an Oklahoma Highway Patrol officer for driving without a license plate and possessing a concealed weapon. Suspicion soon fell on McVeigh due to the circumstantial evidence linking him to the bombing. Investigators traced the rental truck used in the bombing to McVeigh and discovered a wealth of evidence connecting him to the purchase of the bomb's components.

Timothy McVeigh was a former Army soldier who had become increasingly disillusioned with the federal government, particularly following the events at Ruby Ridge in 1992 and the Waco siege in 1993. These incidents, which involved federal law enforcement standoffs with armed civilians, deeply influenced McVeigh's worldview and fueled his anti-government sentiments. He saw the Oklahoma City bombing as a necessary act of retaliation against what he perceived as a tyrannical government.

McVeigh's trial began on April 24, 1997, in Denver, Colorado. The decision to hold the trial in Denver, rather than Oklahoma City, was made due to concerns about finding an impartial jury given the extensive media coverage and the profound impact of the bombing on the local community. The trial was presided over by U.S. District Judge Richard Matsch, a seasoned and respected judge known for his ability to manage complex cases.

The prosecution, led by U.S. Attorney Joseph Hartzler, presented a meticulously detailed case against McVeigh. They outlined the sequence of events leading up to the bombing, provided evidence of McVeigh's preparations, and highlighted his anti-government motivations. The prosecution's evidence included surveillance footage, witness testimonies, and forensic analysis. One of the key pieces of evidence was a receipt for 2,000 pounds of ammonium nitrate fertilizer, which McVeigh had purchased and used to construct the bomb.

Additionally, the prosecution presented emotional testimonies from survivors and families of the victims, painting a vivid picture of the human toll of McVeigh's actions. These testimonies were powerful and served to underscore the gravity of the crime. The prosecution's strategy was to leave no doubt in the minds of the jurors about McVeigh's guilt and the premeditated nature of the attack.

The defense, led by Stephen Jones, faced a daunting task. From the outset, Jones acknowledged the overwhelming evidence against

McVeigh but sought to humanize his client and provide context for his actions. The defense argued that McVeigh was a product of his environment, influenced by his military experiences and disillusioned by government actions at Ruby Ridge and Waco. Jones also attempted to cast doubt on the reliability of certain evidence and the thoroughness of the investigation.

One of the defense's primary arguments was that McVeigh was not acting alone and that others were involved in the bombing. They suggested that McVeigh was part of a larger conspiracy and that the government's case was incomplete. However, the defense struggled to present compelling evidence to support this theory, and their arguments failed to sway the jury significantly.

The trial lasted for nearly five weeks, with both sides presenting their cases in a methodical and comprehensive manner. Throughout the proceedings, McVeigh remained stoic and unemotional, displaying little reaction to the testimonies and evidence presented against him. His demeanor was noted by many observers and contrasted sharply with the emotional testimonies of the survivors and victims' families.

On June 2, 1997, the jury returned a verdict of guilty on all 11 counts, including conspiracy to use a weapon of mass destruction, use of a weapon of mass destruction, destruction with the intent to kill, and eight counts of first-degree murder for the federal law enforcement officers who died in the bombing. The verdict was a decisive victory for the prosecution and a reflection of the strength of the evidence against McVeigh.

The sentencing phase of the trial began shortly after the guilty verdict. The prosecution argued for the death penalty, emphasizing the heinous nature of the crime and the premeditated intent behind it. They presented additional testimonies from victims' families, highlighting the profound impact of the bombing on their lives. The defense, on the other hand, sought to avoid the death penalty by presenting mitigating factors, including McVeigh's military service and his troubled upbringing.

Ultimately, the jury recommended the death penalty, and Judge Matsch formally sentenced McVeigh to death by lethal injection on June 13, 1997. McVeigh was sent to the federal death row at the United States Penitentiary in Terre Haute, Indiana, where he remained for several years. During his time on death row, McVeigh gave several interviews, in which he expressed little remorse for his actions and continued to justify the bombing as a necessary act of retaliation against the government.

Timothy McVeigh was executed on June 11, 2001, becoming the first federal prisoner to be executed since 1963. His execution was carried out with minimal incident, and he maintained his stoic demeanor until the end. McVeigh's last words were a quote from the poem "Invictus" by William Ernest Henley: "I am the master of my fate, I am the captain of my soul." His execution marked the end of a chapter in one of the most tragic and consequential events in American history.

The trial of Timothy McVeigh had far-reaching implications beyond the immediate case. It highlighted the threat of domestic terrorism and the challenges faced by law enforcement in preventing and responding to such acts. The bombing and subsequent trial also led to significant changes in federal policies and procedures, including the establishment of the Oklahoma City National Memorial to honor the victims and the creation of new legislation aimed at combating terrorism.

Moreover, the trial underscored the importance of the judicial system in upholding the rule of law and delivering justice, even in the face of heinous crimes. It demonstrated the capacity of the legal system to handle complex and emotionally charged cases with fairness and due process. The proceedings were closely watched by the public and the media, serving as a testament to the transparency and accountability of the American judicial system.

Chapter 34: The Trial of Oliver North

The trial of Oliver North, a pivotal figure in the Iran-Contra affair, remains one of the most notable and controversial legal proceedings in U.S. history. It shed light on covert operations conducted by the Reagan administration, raised significant constitutional questions, and sparked a national debate about the limits of executive power and accountability in government.

The Iran-Contra affair itself was a complex political scandal that unfolded in the mid-1980s, involving the clandestine sale of arms to Iran, which was then embroiled in the Iran-Iraq War, and the illegal diversion of the proceeds to fund Contra rebels in Nicaragua. These rebels were fighting to overthrow the Sandinista government, which was viewed as Marxist and aligned with the Soviet Union. The scandal broke in November 1986, and subsequent investigations revealed the extent of the secret operations and the involvement of high-ranking officials within the Reagan administration.

Oliver North, a decorated Marine Corps lieutenant colonel, was a National Security Council staff member and played a central role in the operations. North was instrumental in orchestrating the arms sales to Iran and funneling the proceeds to the Contras, despite a congressional ban on such aid known as the Boland Amendment. North's activities were conducted with the knowledge and approval of his superiors, including National Security Advisor John Poindexter and, arguably, President Ronald Reagan himself.

The legal proceedings against Oliver North began after the Tower Commission, appointed by President Reagan, and a subsequent Congressional investigation exposed the details of the Iran-Contra operations. In March 1988, North was indicted on 16 felony counts, including conspiracy to defraud the United States, accepting an illegal gratuity, aiding and abetting the obstruction of a congressional inquiry, and destruction of documents.

North's trial commenced on February 21, 1989, in the U.S. District Court for the District of Columbia, presided over by Judge Gerhard A. Gesell. The prosecution was led by Independent Counsel Lawrence Walsh, a former federal judge and deputy attorney general appointed to investigate the Iran-Contra affair. The prosecution's case rested on demonstrating that North had knowingly violated federal law and obstructed justice in carrying out the covert operations.

The trial garnered intense media attention and was highly politicized. The prosecution presented a wealth of evidence, including documents, memos, and witness testimonies, to establish North's central role in the Iran-Contra operations. One of the most damning pieces of evidence was North's own handwritten notes and memos, which detailed the intricate planning and execution of the arms sales and the diversion of funds. The prosecution also highlighted North's efforts to cover up the operations, including the shredding of documents and providing false testimony to Congress.

North's defense team, led by attorney Brendan Sullivan, employed several strategies to defend their client. They argued that North was acting under orders from his superiors and believed his actions were in the best interest of national security. The defense also contended that the trial was politically motivated and that North was being scapegoated for actions sanctioned by higher authorities, including President Reagan.

One of the most dramatic moments of the trial came when North took the stand in his own defense. During his testimony, North admitted to many of the actions he was accused of but insisted that he was following orders and acting out of patriotic duty. He portrayed himself as a loyal soldier carrying out the directives of his superiors to combat communism and protect American interests. North's testimony was emotional and compelling, and it resonated with many Americans who viewed him as a hero rather than a criminal.

Another critical aspect of the defense was the issue of classified information. North's attorneys argued that much of the evidence against him involved sensitive national security matters that should not be disclosed in open court. They contended that prosecuting North for actions that were part of covert operations could compromise ongoing intelligence activities and jeopardize national security.

Despite these arguments, the jury found North guilty on three of the 16 charges: accepting an illegal gratuity, aiding and abetting in the obstruction of a congressional inquiry, and destruction of documents. On May 4, 1989, Judge Gesell sentenced North to a three-year suspended prison term, two years of probation, 1,200 hours of community service, and a $150,000 fine. The verdict was seen as a mixed outcome, with North avoiding prison time but being held accountable for his actions.

However, North's legal battles did not end with the verdict. In July 1990, the U.S. Court of Appeals for the District of Columbia Circuit vacated his convictions, citing the issue of immunity. North had been granted limited immunity for his congressional testimony, meaning that his testimony could not be used against him in criminal proceedings. The appellate court ruled that the prosecution had failed to demonstrate that its case was not tainted by North's immunized testimony. As a result, the convictions were overturned, and North walked free.

The trial of Oliver North had profound and lasting implications for American politics and law. It exposed the extent of the executive branch's secret operations and the potential for abuse of power. The scandal and subsequent trial underscored the need for greater oversight and accountability of intelligence activities and covert operations. It also sparked a broader debate about the limits of executive authority and the role of Congress in foreign policy and national security matters.

The trial also had a significant impact on public opinion. North emerged from the proceedings with a mixed legacy. To some, he was a patriotic hero who took bold actions to combat communism and protect American interests. To others, he was a symbol of government overreach and the dangers of unchecked executive power. North's trial and the Iran-Contra affair more broadly contributed to a growing cynicism and distrust of government among the American public.

In the years following the trial, North remained a prominent public figure. He became a popular conservative commentator and author, leveraging his notoriety to build a successful media career. He also ran for political office, though his bids for elected office were unsuccessful. North's legacy continues to be a subject of debate and discussion, reflecting the complex and contentious nature of the Iran-Contra affair and its impact on American politics.

The trial of Oliver North is a critical chapter in the history of U.S. governance, highlighting the tensions between national security, executive power, and democratic accountability. It serves as a reminder of the importance of transparency, oversight, and the rule of law in maintaining the integrity of democratic institutions. The lessons of the trial remain relevant today, as the United States continues to grapple with issues of executive authority, intelligence operations, and the balance between security and civil liberties.

Chapter 35: The Trial of Ted Bundy

The trial of Ted Bundy, one of America's most infamous serial killers, stands out as a landmark case in criminal history, drawing intense public and media attention and revealing the complexities of the legal system when dealing with a charismatic and highly manipulative defendant. Ted Bundy's trial journey spanned several years and multiple states, ultimately culminating in his conviction and execution.

Ted Bundy's reign of terror began in the 1970s, spanning across multiple states, including Washington, Oregon, Utah, Colorado, and Florida. Known for his charm and good looks, Bundy lured numerous young women to their deaths, using a variety of methods to gain their trust before abducting, assaulting, and murdering them. His ability to blend in and appear harmless allowed him to evade capture for years, leaving a trail of devastation and fear in his wake.

Bundy's first known arrest occurred in Utah in 1975 when he was pulled over for driving erratically and was found in possession of burglary tools, including handcuffs, an ice pick, and a ski mask. This arrest marked the beginning of a series of legal entanglements for Bundy. During this period, investigators began to link him to a series of unsolved disappearances and murders of young women in the Pacific Northwest. Witnesses and survivors provided descriptions of a man named "Ted," who drove a Volkswagen Beetle, further narrowing down the suspect list.

In 1976, Bundy was convicted of aggravated kidnapping and attempted criminal assault in Utah. He was sentenced to serve time in prison, but his legal troubles were far from over. While incarcerated, Bundy faced additional charges related to the murder of Caryn Campbell in Colorado. In 1977, he managed to escape from a Colorado courthouse by jumping out of a second-story window. Recaptured eight days later, Bundy's audacity and resourcefulness in evading law enforcement only added to his notoriety.

Bundy's most dramatic escape occurred later that same year. On December 30, 1977, he escaped from the Garfield County Jail in Glenwood Springs, Colorado, by crawling through a small hole in the ceiling of his cell and making his way to the jailer's apartment. From there, he walked out the front door and fled. This escape led him to Florida, where he would commit some of his most heinous and well-documented crimes.

In January 1978, Bundy attacked the Chi Omega sorority house at Florida State University in Tallahassee, brutally murdering Margaret Bowman and Lisa Levy, and severely injuring Karen Chandler and Kathy Kleiner. A few weeks later, he abducted and killed 12-year-old Kimberly Leach in Lake City, Florida. These crimes brought Bundy's rampage to a horrifying climax and set the stage for his final capture and trial.

Bundy's arrest in Florida in February 1978 marked the beginning of the end of his criminal career. He was initially apprehended for driving a stolen vehicle, but his identity was soon confirmed, and he was charged with multiple counts of murder, attempted murder, and burglary. The Florida trials would prove to be some of the most significant and highly publicized legal proceedings in American history.

The first trial took place in Miami in 1979, focusing on the Chi Omega sorority house murders. The prosecution, led by Assistant State Attorney Larry Simpson, presented a compelling case against Bundy, relying heavily on forensic evidence and eyewitness testimony. Key pieces of evidence included bite mark impressions found on Lisa Levy's body, which matched Bundy's dental records. Additionally, eyewitnesses identified Bundy as the man they had seen near the sorority house on the night of the murders.

Bundy, who had a background in law and a penchant for self-representation, decided to serve as his own defense attorney. This decision provided a unique and often bizarre spectacle in the courtroom, as Bundy cross-examined witnesses and presented his own legal arguments. His behavior during the trial was erratic, oscillating between charming and aggressive, and his attempts to manipulate the proceedings only served to highlight his narcissism and sociopathy.

Despite his efforts, the evidence against Bundy was overwhelming. On July 24, 1979, the jury found him guilty on all counts, including two counts of first-degree murder for the deaths of Margaret Bowman and Lisa Levy. The verdict was met with relief and satisfaction by the families of the victims and the public at large. During the penalty phase of the trial, the jury recommended the death penalty, which Judge Edward Cowart formally imposed on July 31, 1979. In his sentencing remarks, Judge Cowart famously told Bundy, "You'd have made a good lawyer, and I would have loved to have you practice in front of me, but you went another way, partner."

The second trial took place in Orlando in 1980, this time for the murder of Kimberly Leach. The prosecution, led by Assistant State Attorney Bob Dekle, once again presented a strong case, including testimony from eyewitnesses who had seen Bundy with Leach and forensic evidence linking Bundy to the crime scene. Bundy continued to represent himself, maintaining his innocence and attempting to undermine the credibility of the prosecution's case.

Despite Bundy's best efforts, the jury found him guilty of first-degree murder on February 7, 1980. During the penalty phase, Bundy attempted to sway the jury by portraying himself as a victim of circumstance and by proposing a hasty, impromptu marriage to a former coworker, Carole Ann Boone, who had been one of his supporters throughout his trials. This bizarre spectacle, however, did little to influence the jury, who once again recommended the death penalty. Judge Wallace Jopling sentenced Bundy to death by electrocution on February 10, 1980.

Bundy's conviction and sentencing in Florida marked the culmination of years of legal battles and investigations. However, his case continued to attract attention and controversy. Bundy spent nearly a decade on death row, during which time he pursued numerous appeals and legal maneuvers in an attempt to avoid execution. His appeals primarily focused on procedural issues, such as ineffective assistance of counsel and the admissibility of certain evidence. Despite these efforts, the courts consistently upheld his convictions and death sentences.

Throughout his time on death row, Bundy granted several interviews to journalists and authors, often providing chilling insights into his psyche and the extent of his crimes. In a series of interviews with psychologist James Dobson shortly before his execution, Bundy confessed to additional murders and provided details about his methods and motivations. These confessions further solidified his status as one of the most prolific and depraved serial killers in history.

On January 24, 1989, Ted Bundy was executed in the electric chair at Florida State Prison in Starke, Florida. His execution was witnessed by several reporters and law enforcement officials, and it was met with a sense of closure and justice by the families of his victims and the public. Outside the prison, crowds gathered to celebrate the end of Bundy's life, chanting and holding signs that read "Burn, Bundy, Burn" and "Justice for All."

The trial and eventual execution of Ted Bundy had a profound impact on the American legal system and society. It highlighted the capabilities and limitations of forensic science in criminal investigations, particularly in the use of bite mark evidence, which played a crucial role in Bundy's conviction. The case also underscored the importance of interagency cooperation and communication in tracking and apprehending serial offenders who operate across state lines.

Bundy's trial also brought attention to the psychological and behavioral aspects of serial killers, prompting further research into the minds of such individuals and the development of criminal profiling techniques. The charismatic and manipulative nature of Bundy challenged preconceived notions about what a serial killer looks like, demonstrating that such individuals can often appear outwardly normal and even charming.

Moreover, the extensive media coverage of Bundy's trial and crimes played a significant role in shaping public perceptions of serial killers and the criminal justice system. The sensational nature of the case, combined with Bundy's own courtroom antics and the gruesome details of his murders, captivated the nation and set a precedent for future high-profile criminal trials.

In the years following Bundy's execution, his case has continued to be the subject of extensive analysis and discussion. Numerous books, documentaries, and films have been produced about Bundy's life and crimes, each offering different perspectives on the man and the myth. His case serves as a stark reminder of the capacity for human evil and the challenges faced by the legal system in bringing such individuals to justice.

Chapter 36: The Trial of Jeffrey Dahmer

The trial of Jeffrey Dahmer is one of the most infamous and chilling cases in American criminal history. Known as the Milwaukee Cannibal or the Milwaukee Monster, Dahmer's crimes were so grotesque and unimaginable that they shocked the world. This detailed account will explore the series of events that led to his trial, the legal proceedings themselves, and the broader implications for the criminal justice system and society's understanding of such heinous behavior.

Jeffrey Dahmer's path of destruction began in the late 1970s and continued until his capture in 1991. Over the course of more than a decade, Dahmer murdered 17 young men and boys, engaging in acts of necrophilia, dismemberment, and cannibalism. His modus operandi typically involved luring his victims to his apartment with promises of money or alcohol, then drugging them before carrying out his horrific acts.

Dahmer's early life was marked by a troubled upbringing and signs of deep psychological disturbances. Born on May 21, 1960, in Milwaukee, Wisconsin, Dahmer exhibited odd behavior from a young age. His parents' tumultuous relationship and eventual divorce, combined with his feelings of isolation and alienation, likely contributed to his development into a serial killer. By his teenage years, Dahmer had already begun to fantasize about dominating and controlling others, often imagining elaborate scenarios of sexual violence.

Dahmer's first murder occurred in 1978, shortly after his high school graduation. He picked up hitchhiker Steven Hicks, brought him home, and, after drinking heavily, bludgeoned him to death with a dumbbell. Dahmer dismembered Hicks's body and buried the remains in his backyard. This initial killing set the stage for a decade of escalating violence.

Following his first murder, Dahmer's life was a series of failed attempts at normalcy interspersed with periods of intense, uncontrollable homicidal urges. He enrolled in Ohio State University but dropped out after one term due to poor grades and heavy drinking. In 1979, he joined the U.S. Army and served as a combat medic in Germany. However, his alcoholism led to his discharge in 1981. After his return to the United States, Dahmer's behavior became increasingly erratic.

By the late 1980s, Dahmer had established a routine for his killings. He frequented gay bars and bathhouses, selecting his victims from among the patrons. He often drugged his victims before killing them, allowing him to fulfill his fantasies of complete control. Dahmer's apartment on North 25th Street in Milwaukee became the site of unimaginable horror, filled with the remains of his victims and gruesome trophies of his crimes.

Dahmer's methods of disposing of his victims' bodies were particularly disturbing. He dismembered the corpses, sometimes keeping body parts as souvenirs or for sexual gratification. In several cases, he boiled the flesh off the bones and preserved skulls and genitals in formaldehyde. Dahmer also engaged in acts of cannibalism, consuming parts of his victims to feel a sense of closeness and possession.

The discovery of Dahmer's crimes came on July 22, 1991, when one of his intended victims, Tracy Edwards, managed to escape and flag down two police officers. Edwards led the officers back to Dahmer's apartment, where they were confronted with the stench of decomposition and a scene of unimaginable horror. Upon entering, they found photographs of dismembered bodies and a severed head in the refrigerator. Further investigation revealed a large quantity of human remains, including preserved skulls, bones, and other body parts.

Dahmer was immediately arrested and taken into custody. His confession to the police was both chilling and detailed, as he calmly described the extent of his crimes. Dahmer's admission provided law enforcement with a comprehensive account of his murders, which included not only the number of victims but also the grisly methods he used to carry out and conceal his crimes.

The trial of Jeffrey Dahmer began on January 30, 1992, in Milwaukee, Wisconsin. Due to the overwhelming evidence and Dahmer's own confession, the trial's primary focus was not on determining his guilt but rather on his mental state and whether he could be held criminally responsible for his actions. Dahmer's defense team, led by attorney Gerald Boyle, argued that Dahmer was insane at the time of the murders and, therefore, should not be held fully accountable. They presented evidence of his severe psychological disorders, including necrophilia, borderline personality disorder, and schizotypal personality disorder.

The prosecution, led by Assistant District Attorney E. Michael McCann, countered that Dahmer was fully aware of the wrongfulness of his actions and had gone to great lengths to conceal his crimes, demonstrating a clear understanding of their criminal nature. The prosecution's case was bolstered by the meticulous and calculated manner in which Dahmer carried out his murders, as well as his ability to function in society without arousing significant suspicion.

The trial featured graphic and disturbing testimony from law enforcement officers, medical experts, and survivors. One of the most harrowing moments came when the prosecution presented the photographs and physical evidence found in Dahmer's apartment. The jury was shown images of dismembered bodies, preserved organs, and other macabre items that underscored the sheer brutality of Dahmer's actions.

Dahmer himself took the stand, expressing remorse for his crimes and acknowledging the pain he had caused to the victims' families and

society. He described his compulsions and the uncontrollable urges that drove him to kill, but he also admitted that he understood the wrongfulness of his actions at the time. This admission significantly undermined his insanity defense.

After two weeks of testimony and deliberation, the jury found Jeffrey Dahmer guilty on all counts. On February 15, 1992, he was convicted of 15 counts of first-degree murder. Dahmer was subsequently sentenced to 15 consecutive life terms in prison, amounting to a total of 957 years without the possibility of parole. The sentence ensured that Dahmer would spend the rest of his life behind bars, providing a sense of justice and closure for the victims' families and the broader public.

Following his conviction, Dahmer was transferred to the Columbia Correctional Institution in Portage, Wisconsin. While incarcerated, he was housed in solitary confinement for his own protection due to the high-profile nature of his crimes. Dahmer's time in prison was marked by a mix of hostility and notoriety, as other inmates viewed him with a mixture of fear and fascination.

Despite his heinous crimes, Dahmer's behavior in prison was largely compliant. He expressed a desire to be baptized and became a born-again Christian, seeking redemption for his sins. However, his attempts at rehabilitation did little to change public perception of him as a monster.

On November 28, 1994, Dahmer's life came to a violent end. While performing work duties in the prison gym, he and another inmate, Jesse Anderson, were attacked by fellow inmate Christopher Scarver. Scarver bludgeoned Dahmer to death with a metal bar, delivering fatal blows to his head. Anderson, who had been convicted of murdering his wife, was also killed in the attack. Scarver later stated that he had been disturbed by Dahmer's lack of remorse and the gruesome nature of his crimes.

The trial and eventual death of Jeffrey Dahmer had far-reaching implications for the criminal justice system and society's understanding of serial killers. Dahmer's case highlighted the importance of early intervention and mental health support for individuals exhibiting signs of severe psychological disturbance. It also underscored the need for improved communication and coordination among law enforcement agencies to track and apprehend serial offenders who operate across multiple jurisdictions.

Dahmer's trial also raised important questions about the insanity defense and the criteria for determining criminal responsibility. The case demonstrated the challenges of distinguishing between mental illness and criminal intent, particularly in cases involving such extreme and deviant behavior. The jury's decision to reject Dahmer's insanity plea reflected a broader societal belief in holding individuals accountable for their actions, regardless of underlying psychological disorders.

In the years since Dahmer's trial and death, his case has continued to captivate public imagination and serve as a subject of extensive analysis. Numerous books, documentaries, and films have been produced about Dahmer's life and crimes, each offering different perspectives on the man and the myth. These works have explored the psychological, social, and cultural factors that contributed to Dahmer's development as a serial killer, as well as the impact of his crimes on the victims' families and the community.

One of the most significant aspects of Dahmer's case is its impact on the families of his victims. The trial and subsequent media coverage forced these families to relive the horrors of their loved ones' deaths, often in graphic and painful detail. Many family members have spoken out about the lasting trauma and grief caused by Dahmer's actions, as well as their struggle to find closure and healing in the aftermath of his conviction and death.

Dahmer's case also had a profound effect on the LGBTQ+ community, particularly in Milwaukee. Many of Dahmer's victims were young gay men, and his crimes highlighted the vulnerability and marginalization of this community. The case prompted discussions about the social and cultural factors that contribute to violence against LGBTQ+ individuals, as well as the need for greater protection and support for these communities.

Chapter 37: The Trial of Radovan Karadžić

The trial of Radovan Karadžić stands as one of the most significant and complex legal proceedings of the late 20th and early 21st centuries. It encapsulates the brutal conflicts that tore apart the Balkans in the 1990s, the international community's quest for justice, and the challenges of prosecuting war crimes and crimes against humanity. As the President of the Republika Srpska during the Bosnian War, Karadžić was a central figure in the atrocities that occurred during this period, including the Srebrenica massacre and the siege of Sarajevo. His trial before the International Criminal Tribunal for the former Yugoslavia (ICTY) represented a monumental effort to hold a high-ranking official accountable for genocide and other war crimes.

Radovan Karadžić was born on June 19, 1945, in Petnjica, Montenegro. He pursued a career in psychiatry and poetry before entering politics. His rise to political prominence came as Yugoslavia began to disintegrate in the early 1990s. As the leader of the Serbian Democratic Party (SDS), Karadžić became the first President of the Republika Srpska, a self-declared Serbian entity within Bosnia and Herzegovina. His nationalist rhetoric and policies played a crucial role in the Bosnian War, which lasted from 1992 to 1995.

The Bosnian War was marked by ethnic cleansing, widespread atrocities, and the brutal targeting of civilians. The conflict pitted Bosniaks (Bosnian Muslims), Croats, and Serbs against each other, with each group seeking to secure territory and political dominance. Karadžić and other Serbian leaders pursued a policy of ethnic cleansing to create a homogeneous Serbian state. This involved the systematic expulsion, killing, and imprisonment of non-Serb populations.

One of the most heinous crimes associated with Karadžić was the Srebrenica massacre in July 1995. Srebrenica, an UN-designated safe area, was overrun by Bosnian Serb forces led by General Ratko Mladić. Over the course of several days, approximately 8,000 Bosniak men and boys were systematically executed, and thousands of women and children were forcibly expelled. The massacre was the largest mass killing in Europe since World War II and was later classified as genocide by the ICTY and the International Court of Justice (ICJ).

Another major atrocity linked to Karadžić was the siege of Sarajevo, the capital of Bosnia and Herzegovina. The siege lasted from April 1992 to February 1996, making it one of the longest sieges in modern warfare. During this period, Sarajevo's civilian population was subjected to relentless shelling, sniper attacks, and blockades, resulting in significant loss of life and suffering. The siege aimed to break the will of the Bosnian government and its residents, causing widespread fear and hardship.

The international community's response to the atrocities in Bosnia and Herzegovina was initially slow and inadequate. However, as evidence of ethnic cleansing and mass killings mounted, pressure grew for a decisive response. In 1993, the United Nations established the ICTY, tasked with prosecuting those responsible for serious violations of international humanitarian law in the former Yugoslavia. The tribunal was headquartered in The Hague, Netherlands, and represented a significant step towards international justice and accountability.

Karadžić evaded capture for over a decade after the war, living under various aliases and reportedly receiving assistance from sympathetic networks. However, on July 21, 2008, he was arrested in Belgrade, Serbia, while posing as a new-age healer named Dragan Dabić. His arrest was a major victory for international justice and set the stage for one of the most significant trials in the ICTY's history.

The trial of Radovan Karadžić began on October 26, 2009. He faced 11 charges, including genocide, crimes against humanity, and violations of the laws and customs of war. The indictment covered crimes committed in numerous municipalities in Bosnia and Herzegovina, the Srebrenica genocide, the siege of Sarajevo, and the taking of UN peacekeepers as hostages.

Karadžić chose to represent himself during the trial, although he was assisted by legal advisors. His defense strategy included questioning the legitimacy of the ICTY, denying responsibility for the crimes, and portraying himself as a peacemaker. He argued that his actions were aimed at protecting the Serbian population and maintaining order during a chaotic period.

The prosecution presented a vast array of evidence, including witness testimonies, documents, and forensic reports. Survivors of the Srebrenica massacre and the siege of Sarajevo provided harrowing accounts of their experiences, detailing the brutality and systematic nature of the crimes. Forensic experts presented evidence of mass graves and exhumations, demonstrating the scale of the killings.

One of the key challenges in prosecuting Karadžić was proving his direct involvement and command responsibility for the crimes. The prosecution argued that Karadžić, as the political leader of the Republika Srpska, played a crucial role in planning, orchestrating, and executing the campaign of ethnic cleansing. They presented intercepted communications, orders, and meetings that implicated him in the decision-making process.

The trial also examined the broader context of the conflict, including the role of nationalism, historical grievances, and political maneuvering. Expert witnesses provided insights into the ideological and strategic motivations behind the actions of the Bosnian Serb leadership. The prosecution aimed to show that the atrocities were not random acts of violence but part of a coordinated and systematic effort to achieve ethnic homogeneity.

Karadžić's defense sought to counter these arguments by highlighting the complexity of the conflict and the actions of other parties involved. They argued that the Bosnian government and other factions also committed atrocities, and that Karadžić's actions were a response to these threats. The defense also questioned the reliability of some witnesses and challenged the prosecution's interpretation of evidence.

The trial of Radovan Karadžić was a lengthy and complex process, reflecting the intricacies of international justice and the challenges of prosecuting high-ranking officials for war crimes. It involved extensive legal arguments, procedural issues, and the presentation of vast amounts of evidence. The trial proceedings were broadcast to the public, allowing people around the world to follow the process and understand the gravity of the crimes.

On March 24, 2016, the ICTY delivered its verdict. Radovan Karadžić was found guilty on 10 of the 11 charges, including genocide in Srebrenica, crimes against humanity, and war crimes. He was acquitted of one count of genocide related to crimes in other municipalities. The tribunal sentenced him to 40 years in prison, later increased to life imprisonment on appeal. The verdict marked a significant moment in the pursuit of justice for the victims of the Bosnian War and a reaffirmation of the principles of international law.

The trial and conviction of Radovan Karadžić had profound implications for international justice and the fight against impunity. It demonstrated that even the highest-ranking officials could be held accountable for their actions, sending a strong message that war crimes and crimes against humanity would not go unpunished. The ICTY's work also contributed to the development of international criminal law and set precedents for future cases.

The trial also had a significant impact on the reconciliation process in the Balkans. It provided a sense of justice and closure for the victims and their families, acknowledging the suffering they endured and the crimes committed against them. However, it also highlighted the deep divisions and lingering tensions in the region, underscoring the need for continued efforts towards reconciliation and healing.

Chapter 38: The Trial of Rudolf Hess

The trial of Rudolf Hess, one of Adolf Hitler's closest associates and the Deputy Führer of Nazi Germany, stands as one of the most significant and controversial legal proceedings of the 20th century. As a prominent figure in the Nazi regime, Hess's actions and eventual trial encapsulate the complexities of justice, accountability, and historical reckoning in the aftermath of World War II. His trial before the International Military Tribunal (IMT) at Nuremberg was part of the larger effort to prosecute leading members of the Third Reich for war crimes, crimes against humanity, and crimes against peace.

Rudolf Hess was born on April 26, 1894, in Alexandria, Egypt, to a wealthy German family. He joined the German Army during World War I and was wounded in combat. After the war, Hess became involved in nationalist and anti-Semitic movements, which eventually led him to join the National Socialist German Workers' Party (NSDAP) in 1920. He quickly rose through the ranks, becoming a close confidant of Adolf Hitler. Hess was a key figure in the early development of the Nazi Party, contributing to its ideological foundations and organizational structure.

Hess's role in the Nazi regime was multifaceted. As Deputy Führer, he was responsible for the party's internal affairs and acted as Hitler's personal secretary. He played a significant role in the formulation and implementation of Nazi policies, including those related to anti-Semitism and racial purity. Despite his high position, Hess's influence began to wane as other leaders like Heinrich Himmler and Hermann Göring gained more power. By 1941, Hess had become increasingly marginalized within the Nazi hierarchy.

In May 1941, Hess made a dramatic and puzzling decision that would alter the course of his life and impact his legacy. He flew solo to Scotland in an attempt to negotiate peace with the United Kingdom, hoping to broker an agreement that would allow Nazi Germany to focus its efforts on the Soviet Union. Hess believed that if he could secure peace with Britain, it would strengthen Germany's position in the war. However, his mission was unauthorized by Hitler and was seen as a bizarre and treasonous act. Upon landing in Scotland, Hess was promptly arrested by British authorities and imprisoned for the remainder of the war.

Hess's actions were initially shrouded in mystery, and his motivations for the flight have been the subject of much speculation and debate. Some historians suggest that Hess was driven by a misguided sense of duty and a belief that he could secure peace. Others argue that he was experiencing a mental breakdown and acted out of desperation. Regardless of his reasons, Hess's flight to Scotland effectively ended his active involvement in the Nazi regime and led to his detention as a prisoner of war.

The end of World War II in 1945 marked the beginning of the Allied powers' efforts to bring Nazi leaders to justice. The Nuremberg Trials were established as the primary venue for prosecuting high-ranking officials of the Third Reich. The International Military Tribunal was composed of judges from the United States, the Soviet Union, the United Kingdom, and France. The tribunal aimed to address the unprecedented scale of atrocities committed during the war, including the Holocaust, and to establish a legal precedent for prosecuting war crimes and crimes against humanity.

Rudolf Hess was among the 24 principal defendants at the Nuremberg Trials. The charges against him included crimes against peace, war crimes, and crimes against humanity. Specifically, Hess was accused of conspiring to commit aggression, planning and executing wars of aggression, and participating in the Nazi leadership's overall criminal enterprise. The prosecution aimed to demonstrate that Hess, as a senior Nazi official, bore responsibility for the regime's actions and policies.

The trial began on November 20, 1945, and lasted until October 1, 1946. Hess's defense was complicated by his own behavior and statements. Throughout the proceedings, Hess exhibited erratic behavior and claimed to have amnesia, asserting that he could not remember many of the events and decisions in question. This claim was met with skepticism by both the prosecution and the tribunal. Hess's defense team argued that he was mentally unfit to stand trial, but medical examinations determined that he was capable of understanding the charges and participating in his defense.

One of the central challenges of the trial was establishing Hess's culpability in the broader context of the Nazi regime's crimes. While Hess was not directly involved in the atrocities committed during the Holocaust, his position within the party and his influence on Nazi policy made him complicit in the regime's actions. The prosecution presented evidence of Hess's involvement in the early formation of the Nazi Party, his role in the implementation of anti-Semitic policies, and his participation in the planning and execution of aggressive wars.

Hess's defense sought to portray him as a minor figure who had been sidelined by other, more powerful leaders. They argued that his flight to Scotland was a genuine attempt to negotiate peace and should be seen as evidence of his desire to end the war. The defense also contended that Hess's actions did not directly contribute to the most egregious crimes committed by the Nazi regime. However, the tribunal rejected these arguments, emphasizing the collective responsibility of the Nazi leadership for the regime's crimes.

On October 1, 1946, the International Military Tribunal delivered its verdict. Rudolf Hess was found guilty on two counts: crimes against peace (count one) and conspiracy to commit crimes against peace, war crimes, and crimes against humanity (count two). He was acquitted of war crimes and crimes against humanity (counts three and four). The tribunal sentenced Hess to life imprisonment, citing his prominent role in the Nazi leadership and his involvement in planning and executing wars of aggression.

Following the verdict, Hess was incarcerated in Spandau Prison in Berlin, where he remained for the rest of his life. He spent over 40 years in solitary confinement, becoming the prison's last remaining inmate after other convicted war criminals were released or died. Hess's imprisonment was marked by controversy and debate, with some viewing him as a symbol of Nazi evil and others as a tragic figure who had been unjustly punished.

Rudolf Hess died on August 17, 1987, at the age of 93, in Spandau Prison. His death was officially ruled a suicide by hanging, although conspiracy theories and speculation have persisted regarding the circumstances of his demise. Some have suggested that Hess was murdered to prevent him from revealing sensitive information, while others believe he took his own life out of despair and isolation.

The trial of Rudolf Hess remains a pivotal moment in the history of international law and justice. It underscored the principle that high-ranking officials could be held accountable for their actions and established important precedents for the prosecution of war crimes and crimes against humanity. The Nuremberg Trials, including Hess's case, laid the groundwork for subsequent international tribunals and the development of a permanent International Criminal Court (ICC).

Hess's trial also highlighted the complexities of prosecuting individuals for their roles in large-scale atrocities. The defense's arguments regarding Hess's mental state and the nature of his flight to Scotland illustrate the challenges of determining individual responsibility within the context of a broader criminal enterprise. The trial demonstrated the importance of thorough legal procedures, the presentation of evidence, and the need for impartial judgment in achieving justice.

In retrospect, the trial of Rudolf Hess serves as a reminder of the enduring legacy of the Nuremberg Trials and the ongoing struggle for justice and accountability in the face of crimes against humanity. It also reflects the broader historical context of World War II and the efforts to reckon with the horrors of the Holocaust and the devastation caused by the Nazi regime. The trial remains a significant chapter in the history of international law and a testament to the pursuit of justice in the aftermath of atrocity.

Chapter 39: The Trial of Guy Fawkes

The trial of Guy Fawkes is one of the most famous and dramatic episodes in British history, deeply intertwined with the Gunpowder Plot of 1605. This conspiracy aimed to assassinate King James I and restore a Catholic monarch to the English throne by blowing up the Houses of Parliament during the State Opening. Guy Fawkes, a key figure in the plot, became synonymous with the failed attempt, and his trial and execution have been remembered and commemorated in Britain for centuries.

To understand the trial of Guy Fawkes, it is essential to delve into the political and religious context of early 17th-century England. The country was rife with tension between Protestants and Catholics. After the death of Queen Elizabeth I in 1603, James I ascended to the throne, initially raising hopes among Catholics for greater tolerance. However, James quickly reinforced Protestant dominance, leading to increased persecution of Catholics. This environment of religious strife and political disillusionment set the stage for the Gunpowder Plot.

The conspiracy was masterminded by Robert Catesby, a fervent Catholic who believed that drastic action was necessary to end Protestant rule and bring about a Catholic resurgence. Catesby recruited a group of like-minded conspirators, including Thomas Wintour, John Wright, Thomas Percy, and Guy Fawkes. Fawkes, who had military experience and was knowledgeable in explosives, was tasked with the critical role of handling the gunpowder and executing the plan.

The plotters rented a cellar beneath the House of Lords, and over several months, they secretly transported 36 barrels of gunpowder into the cellar. The plan was to detonate the gunpowder on November 5, 1605, during the State Opening of Parliament, which would kill King James I, the royal family, and numerous members of the aristocracy and government officials. This would create a power vacuum, enabling the conspirators to install a Catholic monarch.

However, the plot was ultimately foiled by an anonymous letter sent to Lord Monteagle, a Catholic nobleman, warning him to avoid the State Opening of Parliament. Monteagle alerted the authorities, who ordered a search of the cellars beneath the House of Lords. On the night of November 4, 1605, Guy Fawkes was discovered guarding the gunpowder. He was immediately arrested and taken to the Tower of London for interrogation.

Guy Fawkes remained stoically defiant during his initial questioning, refusing to reveal the names of his co-conspirators or details of the plot. However, under the intense pressure of torture, which was authorized by King James I himself, Fawkes eventually broke and confessed. The use of torture was a contentious issue, as it was generally illegal in England, but it was deemed necessary given the gravity of the plot. Fawkes endured severe physical pain on the rack, a device designed to stretch the body and dislocate joints, which ultimately forced him to divulge the names of his fellow conspirators and the extent of their plans.

Following his confession, Fawkes and the other captured conspirators were put on trial in January 1606. The trial took place at Westminster Hall, and the proceedings were a public spectacle, attended by a large audience eager to witness the downfall of the notorious plotters. The trial was presided over by Sir Edward Coke, the Attorney General, who presented the evidence against Fawkes and his accomplices. The prosecution argued that the plot was an act of high treason, aimed at overthrowing the government and assassinating the king.

The defendants were charged with conspiring to kill the king, the royal family, and members of Parliament, as well as planning to incite rebellion and restore Catholic rule. The evidence against them included Fawkes's confession, the discovery of the gunpowder, and various incriminating documents. The conspirators, including Fawkes, pleaded not guilty, but their defense was weak and unconvincing.

The trial concluded with a guilty verdict for all the accused. On January 27, 1606, they were sentenced to be hanged, drawn, and quartered, a particularly brutal form of execution reserved for traitors. The punishment involved being dragged on a wooden panel to the place of execution, hanged until near death, then disemboweled, beheaded, and cut into four parts. The gruesome nature of the sentence was intended to serve as a stark warning to anyone contemplating similar acts of treason.

Guy Fawkes and several of his co-conspirators were executed on January 31, 1606. Fawkes's execution took place in the Old Palace Yard at Westminster. As he stood on the scaffold, Fawkes remained resolute and unrepentant. According to contemporary accounts, he managed to jump from the gallows with the noose around his neck, breaking his neck and thus avoiding the agony of the full execution process.

The trial and execution of Guy Fawkes and his fellow conspirators had a profound impact on England. The Gunpowder Plot reinforced the fear and suspicion of Catholics, leading to even harsher measures against them. The English government enacted stricter laws, requiring Catholics to take an oath of allegiance to the king and imposing severe penalties for recusancy, or refusal to attend Anglican services. The plot also intensified anti-Catholic sentiment among the Protestant population, further entrenching religious divisions in the country.

In the years following the trial, the events of November 5, 1605, became a symbolic moment in British history. Parliament declared November 5 as a National Day of Thanksgiving for the plot's failure. The day was commemorated with sermons, bonfires, and fireworks, and it became known as Guy Fawkes Night or Bonfire Night. Effigies of Fawkes, often referred to as "Guys," were burned on bonfires, and the night was marked by celebrations that included the lighting of fireworks.

Over time, Guy Fawkes Night evolved into a more general celebration, losing much of its original anti-Catholic fervor. However, the image of Guy Fawkes and the story of the Gunpowder Plot remained ingrained in British cultural memory. The mask worn by Fawkes, with its distinctive mustachioed visage, became an enduring symbol of resistance and rebellion, famously adopted by the graphic novel and film "V for Vendetta," and subsequently by the hacktivist group Anonymous.

The trial of Guy Fawkes highlights the intense political and religious conflicts of early 17th-century England, as well as the government's efforts to maintain control and suppress dissent. It also underscores the severe measures taken to deal with perceived threats to the state and the lengths to which the authorities would go to ensure their survival. Fawkes's trial and execution served as a stark reminder of the consequences of treason and the brutal reality of justice in an era marked by religious intolerance and political upheaval.

In the broader historical context, the trial of Guy Fawkes can be seen as a pivotal moment that reinforced the Protestant establishment's dominance and solidified the foundations of the modern British state. The failure of the Gunpowder Plot demonstrated the resilience of the government and the determination of the ruling elite to defend their authority against internal threats. It also contributed to the development of a national identity centered around the rejection of Catholicism and the defense of Protestant values.

The enduring legacy of the trial and the Gunpowder Plot continues to resonate in contemporary British culture. Guy Fawkes Night remains a popular annual event, celebrated with bonfires, fireworks, and the burning of effigies. The story of the plot and Fawkes's trial is taught in schools and commemorated in public ceremonies, serving as a reminder of a turbulent and transformative period in British history.

The trial of Guy Fawkes, with its dramatic and gruesome details, captures the imagination and curiosity of people across generations.

It stands as a testament to the complexities of justice, loyalty, and rebellion, and the enduring struggle between authority and resistance. Through the lens of this historical event, we gain insight into the challenges and conflicts that have shaped the course of British history and the ongoing quest for religious and political freedom.

Chapter 40: The Trial of Michael Jackson

The trial of Michael Jackson, officially known as the People v. Jackson, was one of the most high-profile and controversial court cases in the early 21st century. Michael Jackson, the "King of Pop," was accused of child molestation in a case that attracted global media attention and sparked intense debate over his innocence and the nature of celebrity justice. The trial began on January 31, 2005, and ended on June 13, 2005, with Jackson being acquitted of all charges.

The origins of the trial can be traced back to a 2003 documentary titled "Living with Michael Jackson," produced by British journalist Martin Bashir. In the documentary, Jackson openly discussed his practice of allowing children to sleep in his bed at his Neverland Ranch. This revelation led to public outcry and scrutiny, prompting law enforcement to investigate Jackson's interactions with children. The Santa Barbara County District Attorney, Tom Sneddon, who had previously investigated Jackson in 1993 on similar allegations, took a renewed interest in pursuing charges against the pop star.

The 1993 allegations, brought by the family of a boy named Jordan Chandler, had been settled out of court for a reported sum of $20 million. Although Jackson maintained his innocence, the settlement fueled speculation and suspicion about his behavior. The 2003 documentary reignited these suspicions, leading to a new investigation focused on Gavin Arvizo, a 13-year-old boy who had spent time at Neverland Ranch and appeared in the documentary alongside Jackson.

Gavin Arvizo and his family initially defended Jackson, claiming he had helped them during a difficult period in their lives. However, as the investigation progressed, the Arvizo family accused Jackson of molesting Gavin during his visits to Neverland. The accusations included claims of inappropriate touching, providing alcohol to a minor, and attempting to manipulate and control the Arvizo family.

On November 18, 2003, Neverland Ranch was raided by law enforcement officers armed with a search warrant. Investigators combed through Jackson's property, searching for evidence to support the allegations. Jackson was subsequently arrested and charged with multiple counts, including child molestation, administering an intoxicating agent to a minor, and conspiracy to commit child abduction, false imprisonment, and extortion. Jackson vehemently denied the charges, asserting that he was the victim of a conspiracy and a target of extortion.

The trial began in Santa Maria, California, and was presided over by Judge Rodney Melville. The prosecution, led by Tom Sneddon, presented their case by calling numerous witnesses, including Gavin Arvizo, his family members, and former employees of Neverland Ranch. Gavin testified that Jackson had molested him on multiple occasions, describing in detail the alleged incidents of abuse. The prosecution also introduced evidence of prior allegations, including the 1993 case involving Jordan Chandler, to establish a pattern of behavior.

The defense, led by attorney Thomas Mesereau, sought to discredit the Arvizo family's testimony by highlighting inconsistencies and questioning their motives. Mesereau argued that the Arvizo family had a history of dishonesty and financial difficulties, suggesting that they were attempting to exploit Jackson for monetary gain. The defense also pointed out that the Arvizos had previously praised Jackson and expressed gratitude for his support.

One of the key moments in the trial was the testimony of Jackson's former employees, who provided conflicting accounts of their experiences at Neverland Ranch. Some employees claimed to have witnessed inappropriate behavior, while others defended Jackson's character and insisted that he was being unfairly targeted. The defense argued that disgruntled former employees had fabricated stories in an attempt to gain financial compensation or seek revenge against Jackson.

The prosecution introduced evidence, such as adult magazines and alcohol found in Jackson's home, to suggest that Jackson had used these items to groom and manipulate his alleged victims. The defense countered by arguing that the presence of such items did not prove guilt and that Jackson's eccentric lifestyle and behavior were often misunderstood.

Throughout the trial, Michael Jackson's demeanor and appearance were closely scrutinized by the media and the public. He often appeared frail and visibly stressed, leading to speculation about his health and well-being. The trial took a significant toll on Jackson, both emotionally and physically, as he faced the possibility of a lengthy prison sentence and the destruction of his career and reputation.

As the trial progressed, the defense called several high-profile witnesses, including celebrities such as Macaulay Culkin, who testified that they had spent time with Jackson as children and had never experienced any inappropriate behavior. Culkin, in particular, provided strong testimony in Jackson's favor, describing their relationship as innocent and devoid of any misconduct.

The defense also called witnesses who testified about the Arvizo family's credibility and past behavior. They highlighted instances where the Arvizos had been involved in questionable activities, such as a previous lawsuit against J.C. Penney, in which they had accused security guards of assault and later settled for a substantial sum of money. The defense argued that the Arvizos had a pattern of making false accusations for financial gain.

After months of testimony and cross-examination, the trial finally came to a close. The jury, composed of eight women and four men, deliberated for more than a week before reaching a verdict. On June 13, 2005, Michael Jackson was acquitted on all charges. The jury found that the prosecution had failed to prove their case beyond a reasonable doubt and that the evidence presented was insufficient to support the allegations.

The acquittal was met with a mixture of relief and disbelief. Jackson's supporters celebrated his vindication, while critics continued to question his innocence. The trial had exposed the deep divisions in public opinion about Jackson, with some viewing him as a misunderstood and persecuted artist, while others saw him as a potential predator who had escaped justice.

The trial of Michael Jackson had far-reaching implications for both the legal system and the entertainment industry. It highlighted the challenges of prosecuting high-profile cases involving celebrities, where public perception and media coverage can heavily influence the proceedings. The trial also underscored the complexities of child molestation cases, where the credibility of witnesses and the interpretation of evidence play crucial roles in determining the outcome.

For Michael Jackson, the trial marked a turning point in his life and career. Although he was acquitted, the trial had taken a significant toll on his mental and physical health. He became increasingly reclusive and struggled to regain his footing in the music industry. The allegations and the trial's media coverage had irrevocably tarnished his image, casting a long shadow over his legacy.

In the years following the trial, Jackson continued to face legal and financial challenges. He relocated to Bahrain for a period, seeking refuge from the relentless scrutiny of the media. Despite attempts to revive his career, including plans for a comeback tour, Jackson's health continued to deteriorate. He died on June 25, 2009, from acute propofol and benzodiazepine intoxication, a tragic end to a life marked by both extraordinary success and profound controversy.

The trial of Michael Jackson remains a pivotal moment in the history of celebrity justice, exemplifying the intense public fascination and polarization that can accompany cases involving high-profile figures. It serves as a reminder of the complexities and challenges inherent in the legal system, particularly when dealing with allegations of abuse and the powerful influence of fame. The legacy of the trial, much like Jackson's own legacy, continues to be a subject of debate and reflection, revealing the enduring impact of one of the most sensational court cases of the modern era.

Chapter 41: The Trial of Dr. Jack Kevorkian

The trial of Dr. Jack Kevorkian, known as "Dr. Death," was one of the most controversial and highly publicized legal battles in the late 20th century. Kevorkian, a Michigan pathologist, became infamous for his role in advocating and assisting in physician-assisted suicide, sparking a nationwide debate on the ethics and legality of euthanasia. His trial, media coverage, and the broader implications of his actions profoundly impacted discussions on end-of-life care, medical ethics, and the rights of terminally ill patients.

Dr. Jack Kevorkian was born in Pontiac, Michigan, in 1928, to Armenian immigrants. He graduated from the University of Michigan Medical School in 1952 and initially pursued a career in pathology. Over the years, Kevorkian became increasingly interested in the ethics surrounding end-of-life care and euthanasia. His unconventional ideas and methods earned him both notoriety and a dedicated following of supporters who believed in his cause.

Kevorkian's advocacy for physician-assisted suicide began in earnest in the late 1980s. He argued that terminally ill patients should have the right to end their lives with dignity, free from prolonged suffering. To facilitate this, Kevorkian developed a device he called the "Mercitron," which allowed patients to self-administer a lethal dose of medication. His first publicized assisted suicide occurred in 1990, when Janet Adkins, a 54-year-old Alzheimer's patient, used the Mercitron to end her life in a Michigan park. This act thrust Kevorkian into the national spotlight and initiated a series of legal battles that would define his career.

The legality of Kevorkian's actions was immediately called into question. At the time, Michigan had no specific laws prohibiting physician-assisted suicide, but Kevorkian's activities were seen by many as a violation of medical ethics and a dangerous precedent. In response to Adkins' death, the Michigan State Medical Board revoked Kevorkian's medical license in 1991, but this did not deter him. He continued to assist in suicides, claiming to have helped over 130 patients end their lives by 1998.

Kevorkian's activities prompted the Michigan legislature to pass a law explicitly banning physician-assisted suicide in 1993. Undeterred, Kevorkian continued his work, openly defying the new legislation and challenging the authorities to prosecute him. His defiance came to a head in 1998 when he assisted in the death of Thomas Youk, a 52-year-old man suffering from amyotrophic lateral sclerosis (ALS). Unlike his previous cases, Kevorkian directly administered the lethal injection to Youk, rather than using a device that allowed the patient to self-administer the dose.

Kevorkian's decision to personally administer the lethal injection to Youk was a deliberate provocation. He videotaped the procedure and provided the tape to CBS's "60 Minutes," which aired it on national television in November 1998. The broadcast caused an uproar and led to Kevorkian's arrest. He was charged with first-degree murder and the unlawful delivery of a controlled substance. The trial, which began in March 1999, was a culmination of Kevorkian's years of defiance and advocacy for euthanasia.

The prosecution argued that Kevorkian had crossed a line by directly administering the lethal injection, which constituted murder under Michigan law. They contended that his actions were a clear violation of the state's ban on assisted suicide and that he had shown a blatant disregard for the legal and ethical boundaries of medical practice. Kevorkian, who chose to represent himself in court, argued that he was fulfilling a moral and humanitarian duty by helping terminally ill patients end their suffering. He claimed that his actions were motivated by compassion and respect for patient autonomy, not criminal intent.

The trial was highly publicized, with intense media coverage and public interest. Kevorkian's decision to represent himself was seen by many as a strategic move to further publicize his cause and highlight the ethical issues surrounding euthanasia. However, his lack of legal expertise and confrontational style ultimately worked against him. The prosecution presented compelling evidence, including the videotape of Youk's death, which showed Kevorkian administering the lethal injection. This evidence, combined with Kevorkian's own admission of his actions, left little room for doubt regarding his guilt.

In April 1999, the jury found Kevorkian guilty of second-degree murder and the unlawful delivery of a controlled substance. He was sentenced to 10 to 25 years in prison. The verdict was a significant moment in the debate over euthanasia and physician-assisted suicide. It underscored the legal and ethical complexities of end-of-life care and highlighted the limitations of the existing legal framework in addressing these issues.

Kevorkian's conviction sparked widespread debate and drew attention to the broader issues of patient rights, medical ethics, and the role of physicians in end-of-life care. Supporters of euthanasia argued that the verdict was a setback for the right-to-die movement and a denial of patient autonomy. They contended that terminally ill patients should have the right to choose a dignified death, free from prolonged suffering and pain. Critics, on the other hand, argued that Kevorkian's actions were reckless and undermined the integrity of the medical profession. They contended that legalizing euthanasia could lead to abuses and the devaluation of human life.

During his time in prison, Kevorkian continued to advocate for euthanasia and the rights of terminally ill patients. He wrote several books and gave interviews, maintaining his stance that assisted suicide was a compassionate and ethical option for those suffering from incurable diseases. In 2007, after serving eight years of his sentence, Kevorkian was released on parole for good behavior. Upon his release, he vowed to continue advocating for euthanasia but promised to abide by the law and refrain from assisting in any further suicides.

Kevorkian's legacy is complex and contentious. He is regarded by some as a pioneer and a martyr for the right-to-die movement, while others view him as a dangerous maverick who flouted the law and ethical standards of medical practice. His actions and the legal battles that ensued brought the issue of euthanasia to the forefront of public discourse and prompted ongoing debates about the rights of terminally ill patients and the responsibilities of physicians.

The trial of Dr. Jack Kevorkian had a lasting impact on the legal and ethical landscape of end-of-life care. It highlighted the need for clear and consistent legal frameworks to address the complexities of euthanasia and physician-assisted suicide. In the years following Kevorkian's trial, several states in the U.S. have enacted laws legalizing physician-assisted suicide under strict conditions, reflecting a growing recognition of the need to balance patient autonomy with safeguards against potential abuses.

Kevorkian's case also underscored the importance of compassion and empathy in medical practice. It highlighted the ethical dilemmas faced by physicians in caring for terminally ill patients and the need for open and honest discussions about end-of-life care. While the debate over euthanasia and assisted suicide continues, Kevorkian's actions and the legal battles that ensued have contributed to a deeper understanding of the issues at stake and the need for thoughtful and compassionate approaches to end-of-life care.

Chapter 42: The Trial of Amanda Knox

The trial of Amanda Knox, also known as the Meredith Kercher murder case, was one of the most controversial and highly publicized criminal trials of the early 21st century. The case revolved around the brutal murder of British exchange student Meredith Kercher in Perugia, Italy, in November 2007, and the subsequent arrest and prosecution of Amanda Knox, an American exchange student, and her then-boyfriend, Raffaele Sollecito. The trial, media coverage, and legal proceedings spanned several years, characterized by intense scrutiny, legal battles, and fluctuating verdicts.

Meredith Kercher, a 21-year-old student from the University of Leeds, was found dead in the apartment she shared with Amanda Knox and two other women on November 2, 2007. Kercher had been sexually assaulted and brutally murdered, her body discovered in her locked bedroom. The gruesome nature of the crime, coupled with the involvement of international students, quickly drew significant media attention.

Amanda Knox, a 20-year-old student from the University of Washington, had arrived in Perugia to study Italian and European history. She had been living with Kercher for about two months at the time of the murder. Knox's boyfriend, Raffaele Sollecito, an Italian student studying computer engineering, was also drawn into the investigation due to his relationship with Knox and his presence in Perugia.

From the outset, the investigation by the Italian authorities was fraught with controversy. Knox and Sollecito were arrested within days of the discovery of Kercher's body, along with a third suspect, Rudy Guede, an Ivorian immigrant known to local authorities for petty crimes. Guede was eventually found guilty of Kercher's murder in a separate, fast-track trial and sentenced to 16 years in prison.

The case against Knox and Sollecito was built on a combination of forensic evidence, witness testimonies, and circumstantial evidence. However, the prosecution's handling of the case and the evidence presented were subjects of intense debate and criticism.

One of the key pieces of evidence was a knife recovered from Sollecito's apartment, which the prosecution claimed was the murder weapon. The knife had traces of Kercher's DNA on the blade and Knox's DNA on the handle. However, the defense argued that the DNA evidence was contaminated and mishandled by forensic investigators. Additionally, the knife's dimensions did not match the wounds inflicted on Kercher, raising further doubts about its role in the murder.

Another critical piece of evidence was a bra clasp found in Kercher's bedroom, which the prosecution claimed had Sollecito's DNA. This evidence was also contested by the defense, who pointed out that the clasp had been discovered weeks after the initial investigation and could have been contaminated.

The prosecution's case also relied on Knox's behavior and statements during the investigation. Knox initially provided conflicting statements and was accused of falsely implicating her employer, Patrick Lumumba, in the murder. Lumumba was later cleared of any involvement, but Knox's shifting narratives and perceived erratic behavior contributed to the prosecution's portrayal of her as guilty.

The trial of Amanda Knox and Raffaele Sollecito began in January 2009 and was closely followed by media outlets around the world. The prosecution, led by Giuliano Mignini, painted a picture of Knox and Sollecito as cold-blooded killers engaged in a drug-fueled sexual game that resulted in Kercher's death. The defense, on the other hand, argued that Knox and Sollecito were innocent victims of a flawed investigation and media sensationalism.

Throughout the trial, the media coverage was relentless and often sensationalistic. Knox, in particular, was subjected to intense scrutiny, with her behavior, personality, and private life dissected in the press. She was nicknamed "Foxy Knoxy," a moniker that had originally been her soccer nickname but was repurposed by the media to imply a manipulative and cunning personality.

In December 2009, Amanda Knox and Raffaele Sollecito were found guilty of murder and sexual assault. Knox was sentenced to 26 years in prison, while Sollecito received a 25-year sentence. The verdicts were met with shock and outrage by Knox's family and supporters, who believed she had been wrongfully convicted.

Following the conviction, Knox and Sollecito's legal teams launched appeals, arguing that the original trial had been marred by procedural errors and mishandled evidence. In 2011, the case took a dramatic turn when an appeals court in Perugia acquitted both Knox and Sollecito, citing lack of evidence and forensic contamination. Knox returned to the United States, where she was greeted with a mix of support and skepticism.

However, the legal saga was far from over. In 2013, Italy's highest court, the Court of Cassation, annulled the acquittal and ordered a retrial, arguing that the appeals court had not adequately addressed the prosecution's evidence. The retrial took place in Florence in 2014, and once again, Knox and Sollecito were found guilty. Knox was sentenced to 28.5 years in prison, and Sollecito to 25 years.

In 2015, the case reached its final resolution when the Court of Cassation definitively acquitted Knox and Sollecito, citing insufficient evidence and significant flaws in the investigation. The court's ruling underscored the failures of the prosecution's case and the mishandling of forensic evidence.

The trial of Amanda Knox had profound implications for the individuals involved and for the broader legal and media landscape. For Knox, the ordeal was a harrowing experience that lasted nearly a decade, during which she spent four years in an Italian prison. The case highlighted the intense media scrutiny faced by individuals involved in high-profile trials and the potential for miscarriages of justice in the criminal justice system.

The Knox trial also raised questions about the treatment of foreign nationals in the legal system and the influence of media coverage on public perception and judicial proceedings. The sensationalism surrounding the case and the portrayal of Knox as a femme fatale figure were criticized for contributing to a biased and prejudicial environment.

For Meredith Kercher's family, the trial was a long and painful journey in search of justice for their daughter. They expressed frustration with the protracted legal process and the shifting verdicts, which added to their grief and uncertainty. Despite the final acquittal of Knox and Sollecito, the Kercher family continued to seek answers and closure for the loss of Meredith.

The case also had significant implications for the Italian legal system. The handling of the investigation, the reliance on contested forensic evidence, and the lengthy appeals process drew criticism and prompted calls for reforms. The Knox trial underscored the importance of rigorous standards in criminal investigations and the need for fair and impartial judicial proceedings.

In the years following the trial, Amanda Knox has sought to rebuild her life and advocate for criminal justice reform. She has written a memoir, "Waiting to Be Heard," detailing her experiences and the impact of the trial on her life. Knox has also become an outspoken advocate for the wrongfully accused, using her platform to raise awareness about issues related to wrongful convictions and the flaws in the criminal justice system.

The trial of Amanda Knox remains a landmark case in the annals of legal history, serving as a cautionary tale about the complexities of the justice system, the power of media influence, and the enduring quest for truth and fairness in the face of adversity. It is a case that continues to resonate, prompting reflection on the balance between justice and sensationalism, and the human cost of wrongful accusations.

174

Chapter 43: The Trial of Casey Anthony

The trial of Casey Anthony, which captivated the nation and drew intense media scrutiny, is one of the most controversial and sensational legal cases in recent American history. Casey Anthony, a young mother from Orlando, Florida, was charged with the murder of her two-year-old daughter, Caylee Anthony. The case, characterized by its dramatic twists and turns, raised numerous questions about justice, media influence, and the American legal system.

Caylee Anthony was last seen alive on June 16, 2008, but she was not reported missing until July 15, 2008, by her grandmother, Cindy Anthony. Cindy made a frantic 911 call, reporting that her granddaughter had been missing for 31 days and that Casey's car smelled like a dead body. This call set off a chain of events that would lead to one of the most publicized trials in recent memory.

Casey's behavior during the 31 days that Caylee was missing raised immediate suspicions. Instead of reporting her daughter missing, Casey was seen partying, getting a tattoo that read "Bella Vita" (beautiful life), and engaging in a carefree lifestyle. When questioned by the police, Casey initially lied about working at Universal Studios and fabricated stories about a nanny named Zenaida Fernandez-Gonzalez, who she claimed had kidnapped Caylee. These lies quickly unraveled, leading to Casey's arrest on charges of child neglect, making false official statements, and obstructing a criminal investigation.

The investigation into Caylee's disappearance was intense and exhaustive. Search efforts, including volunteer searches and the use of cadaver dogs, were conducted in the hopes of finding the missing toddler. During the investigation, a key piece of evidence was discovered: a car trunk that emitted a strong odor, which forensic experts testified was consistent with human decomposition. Additionally, traces of chloroform and hair similar to Caylee's were found in the trunk. The prosecution would later argue that Casey had used chloroform to sedate Caylee before suffocating her with duct tape.

On December 11, 2008, a meter reader named Roy Kronk discovered Caylee's skeletal remains in a wooded area near the Anthony family home. The remains were found inside a trash bag, with duct tape covering the mouth of the skull. The discovery of Caylee's body intensified the case and added a gruesome element to the already sensational story. The medical examiner concluded that the manner of death was homicide, but the exact cause of death could not be determined due to the advanced state of decomposition.

Casey Anthony was indicted on charges of first-degree murder, aggravated child abuse, aggravated manslaughter of a child, and four counts of providing false information to law enforcement. The trial began on May 24, 2011, and lasted for six weeks, captivating the nation with its dramatic testimonies and media coverage. The prosecution, led by Jeff Ashton and Linda Drane Burdick, argued that Casey had killed Caylee to free herself from the responsibilities of motherhood and pursue a carefree lifestyle. They presented evidence of Casey's lies, her behavior during the 31 days Caylee was missing, and the forensic evidence from the car trunk.

The defense, led by Jose Baez, presented a different narrative. Baez argued that Caylee had accidentally drowned in the family pool on June 16, 2008, and that Casey's father, George Anthony, had helped cover up the accident. The defense claimed that Casey's bizarre behavior and lies were a result of a dysfunctional family environment and alleged sexual abuse by her father. George Anthony vehemently denied these allegations, and no evidence was presented to substantiate the claims of sexual abuse.

One of the most contentious aspects of the trial was the forensic evidence. The prosecution relied heavily on the presence of chloroform in Casey's car trunk and the duct tape found on Caylee's remains. They argued that Casey had researched chloroform on her computer and used it to sedate Caylee. However, the defense countered by questioning the reliability of the forensic evidence and suggesting alternative explanations for the chloroform traces and the smell in the car trunk. The lack of a definitive cause of death also complicated the prosecution's case, as it left room for doubt about how Caylee had died.

Throughout the trial, the defense sought to undermine the prosecution's case by challenging the credibility of witnesses and the interpretation of evidence. They argued that the prosecution had not provided conclusive proof that Casey had murdered her daughter and that reasonable doubt existed regarding the circumstances of Caylee's death. The defense's strategy was to cast doubt on the prosecution's narrative and to present an alternative theory that, while not proven, offered a plausible explanation for Caylee's death.

The trial also featured emotional and dramatic moments, including Casey's mother, Cindy Anthony, breaking down on the witness stand and George Anthony's denial of the defense's allegations of sexual abuse. The intense media coverage and public interest in the case added to the courtroom drama, with reporters and spectators closely following every development.

On July 5, 2011, the jury delivered its verdict after 10 hours of deliberation. Casey Anthony was found not guilty of first-degree murder, aggravated child abuse, and aggravated manslaughter of a child. She was found guilty of four counts of providing false information to law enforcement, for which she was sentenced to time served and was released from jail on July 17, 2011. The not-guilty verdict on the murder charge shocked and outraged many, leading to widespread debate and criticism of the jury's decision and the American legal system.

The trial of Casey Anthony had significant and lasting impacts on the legal and cultural landscape. The case highlighted the challenges and complexities of proving guilt beyond a reasonable doubt, especially in cases with circumstantial evidence and ambiguous forensic findings.

It also underscored the influence of media coverage on public perception and the potential for high-profile cases to become spectacles that blur the line between justice and entertainment.

In the aftermath of the trial, Casey Anthony largely retreated from public view, while the case continued to be a subject of discussion and analysis. Legal experts and commentators debated the strengths and weaknesses of both the prosecution and defense strategies, the role of forensic evidence in criminal trials, and the broader implications of the case for the American justice system.

The trial also had a profound impact on the Anthony family. The allegations and accusations that emerged during the trial strained family relationships and left lasting scars. George and Cindy Anthony, who had been central figures throughout the investigation and trial, faced intense public scrutiny and personal challenges in the years that followed.

Chapter 44: The Trial of Elizabeth Holmes

The trial of Elizabeth Holmes, the founder and former CEO of the health technology company Theranos, is one of the most notable and high-profile cases in recent years, capturing the attention of the media, the public, and the business community alike. Holmes was accused of defrauding investors, patients, and doctors by making false claims about the capabilities of her company's blood-testing technology. The case brought to light significant issues related to corporate governance, investor due diligence, and the ethical responsibilities of technology innovators.

Elizabeth Holmes founded Theranos in 2003 with the vision of revolutionizing the medical testing industry. She claimed that the company had developed proprietary technology capable of running a wide range of tests on just a few drops of blood, which would be faster, cheaper, and less invasive than traditional methods. This promise of a groundbreaking innovation quickly attracted the attention of high-profile investors, including venture capitalists, wealthy individuals, and influential figures such as media mogul Rupert Murdoch and former U.S. Secretary of State Henry Kissinger. By 2014, Theranos was valued at an astonishing $9 billion, and Holmes herself was lauded as a visionary entrepreneur, drawing comparisons to Steve Jobs.

However, behind the scenes, serious issues were emerging. Reports began to surface that Theranos' technology was not as effective or reliable as claimed. Investigative journalist John Carreyrou of The Wall Street Journal played a crucial role in uncovering the truth, publishing a series of articles in 2015 that exposed significant flaws in the company's technology and business practices. Carreyrou's reporting revealed that Theranos had been using commercially available machines for many of its tests, rather than its own technology, and that the results from the company's devices were often inaccurate and inconsistent. These revelations sparked regulatory scrutiny and led to investigations by the U.S. Securities and Exchange Commission (SEC), the Centers for Medicare & Medicaid Services (CMS), and the Department of Justice (DOJ).

In 2018, Holmes and Ramesh "Sunny" Balwani, the former president and COO of Theranos and Holmes' romantic partner, were charged with multiple counts of fraud. The indictment alleged that they engaged in a multi-million dollar scheme to defraud investors and a separate scheme to defraud doctors and patients. The charges included nine counts of wire fraud and two counts of conspiracy to commit wire fraud. Holmes and Balwani pleaded not guilty to all charges, setting the stage for a highly anticipated trial.

The trial of Elizabeth Holmes began in September 2021 and lasted until January 2022. It was held in the United States District Court for the Northern District of California, with Judge Edward Davila presiding. The prosecution, led by Assistant U.S. Attorneys Robert Leach and Jeffrey Schenk, sought to prove that Holmes knowingly and willfully engaged in fraudulent activities to deceive investors and patients about the capabilities of Theranos' technology. The defense, led by attorneys from the prestigious law firm Williams & Connolly, argued that Holmes never intended to deceive anyone and that she believed in the potential of her technology, attributing the company's failures to the complexities and challenges inherent in innovative ventures.

The prosecution's case relied heavily on the testimony of former Theranos employees, investors, and patients who were directly impacted by the company's practices. Key witnesses included former lab directors who testified about the unreliability of Theranos' devices and the pressure they faced to produce favorable results. They described a corporate culture where dissent and concerns about the technology were often dismissed or ignored. Patients and doctors who used Theranos' services also testified about receiving inaccurate test results, which in some cases led to serious medical consequences and unnecessary treatments.

One of the most compelling aspects of the prosecution's case was the extensive documentation of internal emails, presentations, and other communications that illustrated a pattern of deceptive practices. These documents showed that Holmes was aware of the technology's limitations but continued to make public statements and presentations that painted a much rosier picture of Theranos' capabilities. For example, internal emails revealed discussions about the manipulation of data to make the technology appear more effective than it was, and there were instances where Holmes instructed employees to remove problematic data from reports.

The defense, on the other hand, sought to humanize Holmes and portray her as a well-intentioned entrepreneur who was deeply passionate about her company's mission. They argued that Holmes believed in the potential of her technology and that any misrepresentations were not intentional but rather the result of optimism and ambition. The defense also pointed out that Holmes, as a young and relatively inexperienced CEO, relied heavily on the expertise of others, including Balwani and the company's scientific advisors. They suggested that Holmes was not fully aware of all the issues within the company and trusted her team to address them.

Holmes herself took the stand in her own defense, a move that added significant drama to the trial. Over the course of several days of testimony, she recounted her journey in founding Theranos, her vision for the company, and the challenges she faced along the way. She expressed regret for the mistakes that were made but maintained that she never intended to deceive anyone. Holmes also made allegations of emotional and sexual abuse against Balwani, claiming that he exerted control over her personal and professional life, which influenced her decisions and actions. Balwani denied these allegations.

The trial also included testimony from prominent figures who had been involved with Theranos, including former board members and investors. These testimonies highlighted the influence Holmes had in attracting high-profile support and investment, and they illustrated the extent to which she was able to convince experienced and knowledgeable individuals of the viability of her technology. This aspect of the case underscored the persuasive power of Holmes' charisma and vision, which played a significant role in the company's rise and fall.

After months of testimony and deliberations, the jury found Elizabeth Holmes guilty on four counts of fraud: three counts of wire fraud against investors and one count of conspiracy to commit wire fraud. She was acquitted on four counts related to defrauding patients, and the jury was deadlocked on three other counts of wire fraud against investors. Holmes faced a maximum sentence of 20 years in prison for each count, as well as potential fines and restitution. The verdict was a significant moment in the case, marking a rare instance of a high-profile tech executive being held criminally accountable for fraud.

The trial of Elizabeth Holmes had far-reaching implications for the business and technology sectors. It highlighted the importance of due diligence and skepticism on the part of investors, who were shown to have been swayed by Holmes' charisma and the promise of a revolutionary technology without adequately verifying the claims. The case also underscored the need for robust regulatory oversight and accountability in the health technology industry, where the consequences of fraudulent practices can have serious implications for patients' health and well-being.

Furthermore, the trial brought attention to the role of the media in shaping public perception and the pressure faced by entrepreneurs in the high-stakes world of Silicon Valley. The extensive media coverage of the trial, along with the public fascination with Holmes' rise and fall, reflected broader societal interest in issues of corporate ethics, innovation, and the potential pitfalls of the "fake it till you make it" culture often associated with tech startups.

In the aftermath of the trial, Theranos was dissolved, and Holmes' legacy became a cautionary tale about the dangers of overpromising and underdelivering in the pursuit of success. The case also prompted discussions about the responsibilities of founders and CEOs to ensure transparency, honesty, and integrity in their business practices, especially when their products and services have the potential to impact public health and safety.

The trial of Elizabeth Holmes serves as a landmark case in the history of corporate fraud and legal accountability. It offers valuable lessons for entrepreneurs, investors, regulators, and the broader public about the importance of ethical conduct, rigorous oversight, and the need for a healthy dose of skepticism when evaluating claims of groundbreaking innovation. As the story of Theranos and its charismatic founder continues to be analyzed and discussed, it remains a powerful example of how the pursuit of success can lead to ethical lapses with profound consequences.

Chapter 45: The Trial of Derek Chauvin

The trial of Derek Chauvin is a landmark event in the history of the American judicial system and a pivotal moment in the ongoing struggle for racial justice and police reform. Derek Chauvin, a former Minneapolis police officer, was charged with the murder of George Floyd, an unarmed Black man, during an arrest on May 25, 2020. The incident, which was captured on video by a bystander, showed Chauvin kneeling on Floyd's neck for over nine minutes, despite Floyd's pleas that he couldn't breathe. This video sparked global protests and reignited the Black Lives Matter movement, demanding an end to police brutality and systemic racism.

Chauvin faced several charges: second-degree unintentional murder, third-degree murder, and second-degree manslaughter. The trial, held in Hennepin County District Court, began on March 8, 2021, and concluded with a verdict on April 20, 2021. Judge Peter Cahill presided over the case, which drew intense media coverage and public interest worldwide. The prosecution, led by Minnesota Attorney General Keith Ellison, sought to prove that Chauvin's actions directly caused Floyd's death and that his use of force was unreasonable and unlawful.

The prosecution's case was built on several key points. First, they presented the video footage of the incident, which showed Chauvin kneeling on Floyd's neck for an extended period while Floyd repeatedly said, "I can't breathe." This video became a powerful piece of evidence, illustrating the excessive force used by Chauvin and the distress and eventual death of Floyd. The prosecution argued that Chauvin's actions were not only unnecessary but also violated police training and protocols.

Medical experts played a crucial role in the prosecution's case. Dr. Martin Tobin, a pulmonologist, testified that Floyd died from a lack of oxygen caused by the pressure on his neck and back. Dr. Andrew

Baker, the Hennepin County medical examiner, testified that Floyd's death was a homicide caused by cardiopulmonary arrest complicated by law enforcement subdual, restraint, and neck compression. Other medical experts corroborated these findings, emphasizing that Floyd's pre-existing health conditions and the presence of drugs in his system were not the primary causes of his death.

The prosecution also called several police officers and use-of-force experts to testify that Chauvin's actions were not consistent with police training or acceptable practices. Minneapolis Police Chief Medaria Arradondo testified that Chauvin's use of force violated department policies and training, which emphasize the sanctity of life and the importance of de-escalation. Other officers testified that the use of force should have ended once Floyd was no longer resisting and that Chauvin's actions were excessive and unreasonable.

The defense, led by attorney Eric Nelson, argued that Chauvin's actions were justified and that Floyd's death was caused by a combination of factors, including his underlying health conditions and drug use. The defense contended that Floyd's resistance to arrest warranted the use of force and that Chauvin followed his training in applying a knee restraint. They also argued that the presence of fentanyl and methamphetamine in Floyd's system contributed to his death, along with his heart disease.

To support their arguments, the defense called Dr. David Fowler, a former chief medical examiner, who testified that Floyd's death was the result of a combination of factors, including drug use, heart disease, and potential carbon monoxide poisoning from the exhaust of a nearby police vehicle. Fowler's testimony was met with criticism from the prosecution, who argued that it ignored the overwhelming evidence that Chauvin's actions directly caused Floyd's death.

The defense also sought to portray Floyd as a dangerous individual with a history of drug use and criminal behavior, attempting to justify the use of force by Chauvin. However, the prosecution countered this narrative by emphasizing Floyd's humanity and the excessive nature of Chauvin's actions, regardless of Floyd's past.

The trial included emotional testimony from several witnesses who were present at the scene. Darnella Frazier, the teenager who recorded the now-infamous video, testified about the impact the incident had on her and her guilt for not being able to do more to help Floyd. Other bystanders, including an off-duty firefighter and an MMA fighter, testified about their attempts to intervene and their concerns for Floyd's well-being.

The trial concluded with closing arguments on April 19, 2021. The prosecution urged the jury to focus on the video evidence and the expert testimony that demonstrated Chauvin's actions were unlawful and directly caused Floyd's death. The defense reiterated their arguments that Floyd's death was due to a combination of factors and that Chauvin acted within his training and the law.

After ten hours of deliberation, the jury reached a verdict on April 20, 2021. Derek Chauvin was found guilty on all three charges: second-degree unintentional murder, third-degree murder, and second-degree manslaughter. The verdict was met with widespread relief and celebration among those who had been calling for justice for George Floyd. It was seen as a significant step towards accountability for police officers who use excessive force and a validation of the calls for systemic reform.

Chauvin's sentencing took place on June 25, 2021. Judge Peter Cahill sentenced him to 22.5 years in prison for second-degree murder, with the sentences for the other charges running concurrently. The sentence was more than the state guidelines but fell short of the maximum possible sentence. Judge Cahill cited Chauvin's abuse of his position of trust and authority as an aggravating factor in his decision.

The trial of Derek Chauvin has had a profound impact on the national and global conversation about policing, racial justice, and accountability. It highlighted the urgent need for reforms in policing practices, increased transparency, and better training to prevent the use of excessive force. The case also underscored the importance of video evidence in holding law enforcement accountable and the critical role of bystander witnesses in documenting incidents of police misconduct.

In the wake of the trial, there have been renewed efforts to pass legislation aimed at reforming police practices and addressing systemic racism within the criminal justice system. The George Floyd Justice in Policing Act, which seeks to implement comprehensive police reform measures, has been a focal point of these efforts. The act includes provisions to ban chokeholds, create a national registry of police misconduct, and end qualified immunity for law enforcement officers.

The trial of Derek Chauvin also sparked broader reflections on the role of law enforcement in society and the need to reimagine public safety. Activists and community leaders have called for a shift in resources from traditional policing to community-based initiatives that address the root causes of crime, such as poverty, lack of education, and inadequate mental health services.

The trial and its aftermath have had a lasting impact on the legal and social landscape. It has reinforced the importance of accountability and transparency in law enforcement and highlighted the ongoing challenges in achieving racial justice. The case of Derek Chauvin and George Floyd serves as a powerful reminder of the work that remains to be done to create a more just and equitable society.

Chapter 46: The Trial of Harvey Weinstein

The trial of Harvey Weinstein marked a pivotal moment in the #MeToo movement and had far-reaching implications for the entertainment industry and beyond. Weinstein, once a powerful Hollywood mogul and co-founder of Miramax and The Weinstein Company, faced numerous accusations of sexual misconduct, including harassment, assault, and rape, from dozens of women. His downfall began in October 2017 when The New York Times and The New Yorker published exposés detailing decades of alleged sexual abuse and cover-ups. These revelations ignited a global movement against sexual harassment and assault, empowering survivors to come forward with their stories and holding perpetrators accountable.

Weinstein was charged with multiple counts of sexual assault in New York, leading to a high-profile trial that began on January 6, 2020. The charges against him included two counts of predatory sexual assault, one count of criminal sexual assault in the first degree, and one count of rape in the first degree. These charges stemmed from allegations made by two women: Miriam Haley, a former production assistant who accused Weinstein of forcibly performing oral sex on her in 2006, and Jessica Mann, an aspiring actress who claimed Weinstein raped her in 2013.

The trial was presided over by Judge James Burke and held in the New York State Supreme Court. The prosecution, led by Assistant District Attorney Joan Illuzzi-Orbon, presented a case that sought to demonstrate Weinstein's pattern of predatory behavior and abuse of power. The prosecution's strategy involved calling several witnesses, including the two primary accusers and four other women who testified to Weinstein's prior bad acts. These additional witnesses, known as "Molineux witnesses," aimed to establish a pattern of behavior consistent with the allegations.

Miriam Haley testified that Weinstein had invited her to his Soho apartment under the pretext of discussing her career. Once there, she alleged, he forcibly performed oral sex on her despite her repeated objections. Jessica Mann described a similar scenario, recounting how Weinstein raped her in a New York City hotel room. Both women provided graphic and emotional testimony, detailing the fear and trauma they experienced during and after the alleged assaults.

Supporting these testimonies, actress Annabella Sciorra testified that Weinstein had raped her in the early 1990s. Though her accusation was outside the statute of limitations for criminal prosecution, her testimony was crucial in establishing a pattern of predatory behavior. Sciorra's emotional account of the assault and its aftermath provided powerful context for the jury, highlighting the long-lasting impact of Weinstein's alleged actions.

The defense, led by attorneys Donna Rotunno and Damon Cheronis, argued that the encounters were consensual and that the accusers had maintained relationships with Weinstein after the alleged incidents. They sought to discredit the accusers by pointing to friendly emails and interactions they had with Weinstein post-assault. The defense's strategy was to paint Weinstein's accusers as opportunistic and to suggest that the allegations were part of a larger, misguided #MeToo crusade against him.

One of the defense's key arguments centered on the credibility of the accusers and the complexities of human relationships. They emphasized that consensual relationships can sometimes involve problematic dynamics and that the accusers' continued contact with Weinstein was evidence of consensual relationships, not coercion or assault. The defense also argued that the prosecution's reliance on emotional testimony was meant to evoke sympathy rather than provide concrete evidence of criminal behavior.

The trial featured contentious cross-examinations, with the defense questioning the accusers' motives and the consistency of their accounts. The prosecution, in turn, highlighted the power imbalance between Weinstein and his accusers, arguing that his influence and control in Hollywood made it difficult for the women to come forward sooner or sever ties with him completely.

The jury, composed of seven men and five women, faced the challenging task of weighing the conflicting narratives and determining the credibility of the testimonies. After five days of deliberation, the jury reached a verdict on February 24, 2020. Weinstein was found guilty of two charges: criminal sexual assault in the first degree for the assault on Miriam Haley and rape in the third degree for the assault on Jessica Mann. He was acquitted of the most serious charges of predatory sexual assault, which would have required proof of a pattern of predatory behavior.

Weinstein's conviction was met with widespread approval and seen as a significant victory for the #MeToo movement. It was a moment of validation for the survivors who had bravely come forward and a clear message that powerful men could be held accountable for their actions. The verdict also underscored the importance of believing survivors and the role of the judicial system in addressing sexual violence.

On March 11, 2020, Weinstein was sentenced to 23 years in prison by Judge James Burke. The sentence was significant, reflecting the severity of the crimes and the impact on the victims. Judge Burke emphasized that Weinstein's actions were not only criminal but also an egregious abuse of power. The sentence served as a stark reminder of the consequences of using power and influence to exploit and harm others.

Weinstein's trial and conviction had far-reaching implications beyond the courtroom. It galvanized the #MeToo movement, inspiring more survivors to come forward and share their stories. It also prompted a broader conversation about consent, power dynamics, and accountability in various industries. The entertainment industry, in particular, faced increased scrutiny and calls for systemic changes to prevent harassment and abuse.

In the aftermath of the trial, several organizations and institutions implemented measures to address sexual misconduct and support survivors. The Time's Up movement, founded in response to the Weinstein scandal, continued its advocacy for safer workplaces and legal support for victims of sexual harassment and assault. Hollywood studios and production companies adopted stricter policies and guidelines to prevent misconduct and create a culture of respect and accountability.

Weinstein's case also influenced legal and legislative efforts to combat sexual violence. Lawmakers in various states introduced bills to extend the statute of limitations for sexual assault cases, increase penalties for sexual crimes, and provide more support for survivors. The trial highlighted the need for comprehensive reforms to address the systemic issues that allow predators to operate with impunity.

The cultural impact of Weinstein's trial was profound, shifting societal attitudes towards sexual misconduct and reinforcing the importance of accountability and justice. It demonstrated that even the most powerful individuals could be held responsible for their actions and that survivors' voices could affect meaningful change. The trial also underscored the role of the media in exposing wrongdoing and amplifying the voices of those who have been silenced.

Despite his conviction, Weinstein faced additional legal challenges. He was indicted on similar charges in Los Angeles, where he awaited extradition and trial. These charges, related to incidents in 2013, further underscored the widespread nature of his alleged misconduct and the continuing efforts to hold him accountable.

The trial of Harvey Weinstein stands as a landmark case in the fight against sexual violence and a testament to the resilience and courage of survivors. It brought to light the pervasive issue of sexual misconduct in powerful industries and underscored the need for ongoing efforts to ensure justice and support for those affected by such crimes. The trial and its aftermath continue to shape the conversation around sexual violence, power, and accountability, reinforcing the importance of vigilance and advocacy in the pursuit of a safer and more equitable society.

Chapter 47: The Trial of the Pendle Witches

The Trial of the Pendle Witches, which took place in 1612, is one of the most famous and well-documented witchcraft trials in English history. It provides a fascinating and chilling insight into the superstitions, social tensions, and judicial practices of the early 17th century. The trial resulted in the execution of ten individuals from the area around Pendle Hill in Lancashire, accused of practicing witchcraft and causing harm through magical means.

The story begins in the rural and economically depressed region of Pendle Hill, where suspicions and accusations of witchcraft were not uncommon. The area had a long history of folklore and belief in the supernatural, which was further fueled by the general climate of fear and paranoia that characterized much of Europe during this period. The trial was sparked by a series of events involving members of two rival families, the Demdikes and the Chattoxes, who were reputed to be practitioners of witchcraft.

The initial accusations arose when Alizon Device, a member of the Demdike family, was accused of bewitching John Law, a pedlar who claimed to have been struck down by a mysterious illness after a confrontation with her. Law's son took the matter to the local magistrate, Roger Nowell, who began an investigation that quickly escalated. Alizon confessed to being a witch and implicated others, including her grandmother, Elizabeth Southerns (known as Old Demdike), and members of the rival Chattox family, led by Anne Whittle (Old Chattox).

Roger Nowell's investigation was thorough and determined, reflecting the seriousness with which accusations of witchcraft were treated at the time. He gathered testimonies from various individuals who claimed to have suffered harm or witnessed suspicious activities.

The suspects were interrogated, and their confessions were extracted under conditions that would likely be considered coercive today. Old Demdike and Old Chattox both confessed to witchcraft, recounting their supposed dealings with familiar spirits and their participation in dark rituals.

The case took on a life of its own as more accusations surfaced. The two families were deeply intertwined through a network of relationships and mutual suspicions, and the investigation soon expanded to include others in the community. Among those accused were Alizon's mother, Elizabeth Device, her brother, James Device, and Anne Redferne, the daughter of Old Chattox. The evidence against them was often based on hearsay, personal grudges, and the confessions of the accused themselves, many of whom were likely seeking to avoid further torture or gain some leniency.

One particularly damning piece of evidence was the testimony of a young girl, Jennet Device, the nine-year-old daughter of Elizabeth Device. Jennet's testimony was pivotal in the trial, as she confidently pointed out her mother, brother, and other relatives as witches. Her testimony was given significant weight by the court, despite her young age, and it played a crucial role in securing the convictions of several of the accused. The use of a child as a key witness highlights the desperation and fervor with which witchcraft accusations were pursued.

The trial was held at Lancaster Assizes in August 1612, presided over by Sir James Altham and Sir Edward Bromley. The accused were charged with various acts of witchcraft, including causing death and illness through supernatural means, using spells and charms, and consorting with familiar spirits. The legal proceedings were conducted with a mix of common law practices and the specific statutes against witchcraft, which were harsh and often relied heavily on confessions and witness testimonies.

One of the most notorious aspects of the trial was the condition of the accused during their imprisonment and trial. The prisoners were held in the dungeon of Lancaster Castle, a dark and damp place that exacerbated their suffering. Many of them were already elderly and in poor health, and the conditions of their confinement likely contributed to their weakened state and willingness to confess.

The trial culminated in a series of dramatic and emotional confrontations. Elizabeth Device, in particular, drew attention for her outbursts and vehement denials. She was described as a "malicious, wicked creature," and her demeanor was used against her as evidence of her guilt. The trial proceedings were heavily biased against the accused, with the judges and prosecutors framing their actions within the prevailing beliefs about witchcraft and demonic possession.

In the end, ten of the accused were found guilty and sentenced to death by hanging. These included Alizon Device, Elizabeth Device, James Device, Anne Whittle (Old Chattox), Anne Redferne, Alice Nutter, Katherine Hewitt, John Bulcock, Jane Bulcock, and Isobel Robey. Their executions took place on August 20, 1612, at Gallows Hill in Lancaster, bringing a tragic end to the lives of those who had been caught up in the hysteria and fear of the time.

The Pendle Witch Trials have been remembered and studied for centuries as a stark example of the dangers of superstition, scapegoating, and the misuse of judicial power. They reveal the extent to which fear and ignorance could fuel accusations and lead to the persecution of innocent people. The trials also highlight the role of social and economic factors in the dynamics of witchcraft accusations, as many of the accused were poor, marginalized individuals living on the fringes of society.

In the years following the trial, the story of the Pendle Witches became part of local folklore and national history. It has been the subject of numerous books, plays, and studies, each seeking to understand and interpret the events from various perspectives. The trials have also been commemorated in the Pendle Witch Trail, a walking route that takes visitors through the sites associated with the accused witches, offering a poignant reminder of the historical events and their enduring legacy.

The trial of the Pendle Witches serves as a cautionary tale about the consequences of mass hysteria, the importance of due process and fairness in judicial proceedings, and the need to guard against the dehumanization of those who are different or marginalized. It stands as a testament to the resilience of the human spirit in the face of injustice and the enduring impact of historical events on collective memory and cultural identity.

Through the lens of the Pendle Witch Trials, we can better understand the broader context of witchcraft persecution in early modern Europe, where thousands of people, mostly women, were accused, tortured, and executed. The trials reflect the interplay of fear, power, and social dynamics that fueled the witch hunts and offer valuable lessons for contemporary discussions about justice, human rights, and the dangers of unchecked authority.

The legacy of the Pendle Witches continues to resonate today, serving as a reminder of the importance of vigilance against the forces of fear and prejudice and the necessity of upholding principles of justice and humanity in all aspects of society.

Chapter 48: The Trial of Louis Riel

The Trial of Louis Riel is one of the most significant and controversial legal proceedings in Canadian history. It involved the prosecution of Louis Riel, a political and spiritual leader of the Métis people, who played a crucial role in the Red River and North-West Rebellions. His trial, which took place in 1885, not only highlighted the complex relationship between the Canadian government and Indigenous peoples but also underscored issues of national identity, cultural survival, and justice.

Louis Riel was born in 1844 in the Red River Settlement (present-day Manitoba) to a Métis family. The Métis are a distinct cultural group with mixed Indigenous and European ancestry. From a young age, Riel was identified as a promising student and was sent to study in Montreal. Despite his potential for a career in the church or law, he returned to Red River at the age of 24 to become involved in the political struggles of his people.

The first significant political action led by Riel was the Red River Rebellion of 1869-1870. When the Canadian government, eager to expand its territory westward, sought to purchase the vast lands of Rupert's Land from the Hudson's Bay Company, the Métis feared for their land rights, culture, and way of life. Riel established a provisional government to negotiate with the Canadian authorities and ultimately succeeded in securing significant concessions, including the creation of the province of Manitoba through the Manitoba Act, which promised land rights and cultural protections for the Métis. However, his involvement in the execution of Thomas Scott, an Orangeman who opposed the Métis government, made him a polarizing figure and led to his exile from Canada for several years.

Riel's second major involvement in Métis resistance came with the North-West Rebellion of 1885. By this time, the Métis had migrated westward into present-day Saskatchewan, where they again found their land rights under threat from the Canadian government's policies favoring European settlers and the construction of the Canadian Pacific Railway. Riel returned from the United States, where he had been living, to lead the Métis in their struggle for recognition and rights. His leadership in the armed resistance against Canadian forces culminated in several battles, most notably the Battle of Batoche, where the Métis forces were ultimately defeated.

Following the defeat, Riel surrendered and was taken to Regina, where he was put on trial for high treason. The trial, which began on July 20, 1885, was conducted in an atmosphere of considerable tension and political pressure. The charge of high treason was a serious one, and the trial was seen as a test of the Canadian government's authority and its ability to deal with dissidence within its territories.

The legal proceedings were fraught with controversy from the outset. Riel's defense team, composed of Charles Fitzpatrick, François-Xavier Lemieux, and others, faced significant challenges. The trial judge, Hugh Richardson, and the jury, which consisted entirely of English-speaking Protestants, were perceived to be biased against Riel, a Catholic and a Francophone. Furthermore, the political context influenced the proceedings, as Prime Minister John A. Macdonald's government was keen to assert its control over the western territories and suppress any further resistance.

One of the key strategies of the defense was to plead insanity. Riel had exhibited signs of mental instability in the past, including periods of delusion where he believed he was divinely inspired to lead his people. His defense counsel argued that he was not responsible for his actions during the rebellion due to his mental state. However, Riel himself rejected this defense, insisting on his sanity and taking the opportunity to present a political justification for his actions. He argued that his resistance was a legitimate struggle for the rights and survival of the Métis people against a government that was violating their rights and failing to uphold its promises.

The trial featured numerous witnesses and extensive testimony, both from those who supported Riel and those who opposed him. The prosecution, led by Christopher Robinson and Britton Bath Osler, focused on portraying Riel as a dangerous rebel who had instigated a violent uprising against lawful authority. They presented evidence of his leadership in the armed resistance and his proclamations as a means to prove his intent to overthrow the government.

Despite the efforts of the defense to provide context for Riel's actions and to challenge the legitimacy of the government's policies, the jury found Riel guilty of high treason on August 1, 1885. The mandatory sentence for high treason was death by hanging. The verdict and the sentence sparked a heated debate across Canada. Many French Canadians and Catholics viewed Riel as a martyr and a defender of minority rights, while English Canadians and Protestants largely saw him as a traitor who had challenged the authority of the state.

Following the verdict, there were numerous appeals for clemency. Riel's defense team, his supporters, and various political figures argued for a commutation of his sentence on grounds of his mental state and the broader political implications of executing him. However, Prime Minister Macdonald and his government were determined to make an example of Riel to deter any future rebellions. Macdonald famously remarked, "He shall hang, though every dog in Quebec bark in his favour."

Riel was executed by hanging on November 16, 1885. His execution had profound and lasting repercussions. It intensified the already deep divisions between French and English Canadians, contributing to a sense of alienation and grievance among French Canadians that would have long-term implications for Canadian unity. For the Métis, Riel became a symbol of their struggle for recognition and rights, and his legacy continues to be celebrated by Indigenous and Francophone communities.

The trial of Louis Riel remains a pivotal moment in Canadian history, representing a clash between different visions of the nation and highlighting the challenges of governance in a diverse and expanding country. It underscores the complexities of justice and the influence of political considerations in legal proceedings. Riel's life and trial have been the subject of extensive historical and cultural examination, inspiring numerous books, plays, and academic studies. His legacy as a defender of his people and a visionary leader who sought to bridge cultural divides and advocate for justice continues to resonate in contemporary discussions about Indigenous rights and national identity in Canada.

The trial of Louis Riel thus stands as a powerful reminder of the ongoing struggle for justice and equality in the face of political and social challenges. It serves as a testament to the enduring impact of historical events on collective memory and the shaping of national narratives. As Canada continues to grapple with issues of reconciliation and the rights of Indigenous peoples, the story of Louis Riel offers important lessons about the importance of understanding and respecting diverse perspectives and the need for a just and inclusive society.

Chapter 49: The Trial of Marie Antoinette

The trial of Marie Antoinette, the last Queen of France before the fall of the monarchy during the French Revolution, is one of the most dramatic and historically significant episodes in the tumultuous period of the late 18th century. This trial not only marked the end of an era for the French monarchy but also epitomized the intense political and social upheaval that characterized the Revolution. The trial, held in October 1793, was a culmination of years of mounting public hatred, political intrigue, and revolutionary fervor.

Marie Antoinette, born an Archduchess of Austria in 1755, married Louis-Auguste, the future King Louis XVI of France, at the age of 14. Her marriage was intended to strengthen the alliance between Austria and France, two powerful European dynasties. However, her foreign birth and lavish lifestyle quickly made her a target of public disdain. As France faced financial crises, partly due to its involvement in the American Revolution, the royal family's extravagant expenditures became a focal point of criticism, and Marie Antoinette was pejoratively dubbed "Madame Déficit."

Her trial was a direct consequence of the French Revolution, which began in 1789 with the storming of the Bastille and escalated with the establishment of the National Assembly and the subsequent execution of her husband, King Louis XVI, in January 1793. Following the king's execution, Marie Antoinette's fate was precarious. Imprisoned in the Temple Tower with her children, her brother-in-law, and other members of the royal household, she was a prisoner of the Revolution, a symbol of the old regime the revolutionaries sought to dismantle.

By the time of her trial, the political climate in France was extremely volatile. The Reign of Terror, led by the radical Jacobins and their leader Maximilien Robespierre, was in full swing. Thousands of people were executed as suspected enemies of the Revolution. The Revolutionary Tribunal, established to try these enemies, became the primary tool of the Jacobins' ruthless campaign to consolidate power and eliminate opposition. In this context, the trial of Marie Antoinette was not merely a legal proceeding but a politically charged spectacle designed to justify the Revolution and demonize the ancien régime.

The trial began on October 14, 1793. Marie Antoinette, now known simply as "the Widow Capet," was 37 years old but appeared much older due to the severe conditions of her imprisonment and the emotional strain of losing her husband and being separated from her children. The charges against her were numerous and varied, reflecting both political accusations and personal animosities. Among the principal charges were depleting the national treasury, conspiracy against the security of the state, and high treason. Particularly sensational were the charges of sexual depravity, including an accusation by her son Louis Charles, possibly coerced, that she had sexually abused him. This latter charge was meant to humiliate her and turn public sentiment further against her, although she vehemently denied it in a powerful rebuttal that reportedly moved some of the women in the courtroom to tears.

The prosecution, led by Antoine Quentin Fouquier-Tinville, relied heavily on circumstantial evidence, rumors, and the general unpopularity of Marie Antoinette. The proceedings were far from impartial; they were a formality leading to a predetermined conclusion. The Queen's defense attorneys, Claude François Chauveau-Lagarde and Guillaume Alexandre Tronson du Coudray, had little chance to mount an effective defense in the face of overwhelming public hostility and a tribunal bent on securing a conviction. They argued that the charges were exaggerated or unproven and highlighted her role as a mother and a queen who had been following the interests of her husband and her adopted country.

Despite their efforts, the outcome was never in doubt. After two days of testimony and limited deliberation, the tribunal found her guilty on all counts. On October 16, 1793, Marie Antoinette was sentenced to death by guillotine. Her composure and dignity during her final hours left a lasting impression on many of her contemporaries and have been the subject of much historical reflection.

On the day of her execution, Marie Antoinette was taken in a common cart through the streets of Paris, facing a hostile crowd. Her once luxurious hair was cut short, and she wore a plain white dress. According to reports, she maintained her composure and remained dignified despite the jeers and insults from the crowd. Upon reaching the Place de la Révolution, she was led up the steps to the guillotine. Her final words were an apology to her executioner, Henri Sanson, for stepping on his foot: "Pardon me, sir, I did not do it on purpose."

Marie Antoinette's execution marked the symbolic end of the French monarchy and the triumph of the Revolution over the old order. Her death, however, also had a profound impact on the Revolution itself. It demonstrated the Revolution's radical shift from its original ideals of liberty and equality to a period characterized by extreme violence and political purges. The execution of the Queen, along with the thousands of others during the Reign of Terror, contributed to growing disillusionment and fear among the French populace, ultimately leading to the downfall of the Jacobins and the rise of more moderate revolutionary leaders.

In the years following her death, Marie Antoinette's legacy has been the subject of intense debate and reevaluation. To some, she remains a symbol of the excesses and failings of the French monarchy, an out-of-touch foreign queen who contributed to her own downfall through her extravagant lifestyle and political naiveté. To others, she is a tragic figure, a scapegoat for the broader systemic issues facing France, and a victim of political and personal animosity. Her life and trial continue to fascinate historians, authors, and the public, reflecting the complex and often contradictory nature of her character and her historical significance.

The trial of Marie Antoinette thus stands as a critical moment in the history of the French Revolution, encapsulating the period's intense political and social transformations. It highlights the ways in which justice can be influenced by broader societal forces and underscores the enduring impact of individual lives on the course of history. Marie Antoinette's trial and execution remain a poignant reminder of the human costs of political upheaval and the relentless pursuit of revolutionary ideals.

Chapter 50: The Trial of Clive Ponting

The trial of Clive Ponting, a senior civil servant in the British Ministry of Defence, is a significant moment in the history of British legal and political culture. This trial took place in the mid-1980s and revolved around issues of governmental transparency, public interest, and the role of whistleblowers. Ponting's case drew widespread attention and sparked a national debate about the balance between state secrecy and democratic accountability.

Clive Ponting was a high-ranking official with considerable experience in the Ministry of Defence. He came into the public eye due to his involvement in the controversy surrounding the sinking of the Argentine warship General Belgrano during the Falklands War in 1982. The sinking of the Belgrano, which resulted in the loss of 323 lives, was a critical and contentious episode in the conflict between the United Kingdom and Argentina over the Falkland Islands.

Initially, the British government, led by Prime Minister Margaret Thatcher, justified the sinking by claiming that the Belgrano was a legitimate threat to British forces. However, as details emerged, doubts were raised about whether the ship was actually moving towards the British task force when it was attacked, or if it was, in fact, sailing away from the conflict zone. This discrepancy became a focal point of public and parliamentary scrutiny.

Ponting, who had access to classified information, discovered documents that contradicted the government's official narrative. He found that the Belgrano was indeed sailing away from the Falkland Islands exclusion zone when it was torpedoed by a British submarine. Ponting believed that the public and Parliament had the right to know the truth about this significant military action. In an act of conscience, he decided to leak the documents to Tam Dalyell, a Labour Member of Parliament who was an outspoken critic of the government's handling of the Falklands War.

The leak, which occurred in 1984, created a storm of controversy. Dalyell used the information to challenge the government's version of events, accusing it of misleading Parliament and the public. The Thatcher government, determined to maintain its narrative and protect its authority, responded with severe measures. Ponting was identified as the source of the leak, and in an unprecedented move, he was charged under Section 2 of the Official Secrets Act of 1911. This section made it an offence to disclose information without lawful authority.

The trial of Clive Ponting began in February 1985 at the Old Bailey, London's central criminal court. The prosecution argued that Ponting had breached the Official Secrets Act by leaking classified documents and that his actions endangered national security. The case was prosecuted by Sir Thomas Hetherington, the Director of Public Prosecutions, and featured evidence and arguments that underscored the government's stance on maintaining strict control over sensitive information.

Ponting's defence was built around the notion of public interest. His lawyer, Michael Mansfield QC, argued that Ponting had acted out of a sense of duty to inform Parliament and the public about a matter of significant public interest. The defence contended that the information leaked did not pose a genuine threat to national security but instead exposed the government's duplicity.

One of the key aspects of the trial was the jury's perception of the role of civil servants and the ethical considerations surrounding whistleblowing. Ponting's defence team highlighted his integrity and sense of moral responsibility, portraying him as a principled individual standing up against governmental wrongdoing. The trial brought into sharp focus the conflict between legal obligations under the Official Secrets Act and the ethical duty to expose misconduct.

The case took a dramatic turn when Ponting took the stand to testify in his own defence. He argued eloquently that his actions were motivated by a desire to ensure that the government was held accountable for its actions. Ponting's testimony resonated with the jury, who were confronted with the ethical dilemma of whether upholding the law should always take precedence over revealing the truth in matters of public importance.

The trial concluded with a remarkable verdict. Despite the clear evidence that Ponting had breached the Official Secrets Act, the jury acquitted him. The jury's decision was seen as a victory for transparency and accountability, highlighting the importance of the public's right to know and the role of individuals in safeguarding democratic principles. The acquittal sent a powerful message that the jury did not view Ponting's actions as criminal but as a necessary act of whistleblowing in the public interest.

The aftermath of the trial had significant implications for British politics and the legal system. The Thatcher government was deeply embarrassed by the outcome, which undermined its authority and raised questions about its commitment to transparency. The case also led to a broader debate about the Official Secrets Act and the need for legal reforms to protect whistleblowers who act in the public interest.

In the years following the trial, the debate over the balance between state secrecy and public accountability continued. The Public Interest Disclosure Act of 1998 was introduced to provide legal protection for whistleblowers, although it did not completely resolve the tensions highlighted by Ponting's case. The act was designed to encourage individuals to report misconduct without fear of reprisal, reflecting a growing recognition of the importance of whistleblowing in promoting transparency and accountability.

The trial of Clive Ponting remains a landmark case in the history of British justice. It exemplifies the challenges faced by individuals who confront governmental secrecy and underscores the vital role of whistleblowers in a democratic society. Ponting's courage and the jury's verdict serve as enduring reminders of the ethical complexities inherent in balancing national security with the public's right to know the truth.

The case continues to be studied and debated as a pivotal moment that shaped the discourse on governmental transparency and the protection of whistleblowers.

Epilogue

As we reach the conclusion of "The Historical Verdicts: Pivotal Court Cases Through History," we find ourselves standing at the intersection of past and present, where the echoes of landmark trials reverberate through time. The stories of these fifty cases have taken us on a journey through the complexities of human nature, the evolution of societal norms, and the relentless pursuit of justice. Each verdict, whether celebrated or contested, has contributed to the legal and moral fabric of our world.

Throughout this exploration, we have witnessed how courtroom battles can transcend their immediate circumstances, influencing future generations and reshaping the trajectory of history. The trials of Socrates, Joan of Arc, and Galileo Galilei remind us of the enduring struggle for intellectual freedom and the courage to challenge prevailing orthodoxy. The cases of Brown v. Board of Education and Roe v. Wade highlight the ongoing quest for civil rights and personal autonomy. The trials of Nelson Mandela and the Nuremberg defendants underscore the global fight against oppression and the pursuit of accountability for crimes against humanity.

These historical verdicts also serve as powerful reminders of the law's potential to both uphold and undermine justice. They illustrate how legal systems, while designed to arbitrate fairness, are not immune to the biases, prejudices, and power dynamics of their times. The wrongful convictions and miscarriages of justice that we have examined underscore the importance of continual vigilance, reform, and the unwavering commitment to truth.

As we look to the future, the lessons from these pivotal court cases remain ever relevant. The challenges faced by past generations in their pursuit of justice are mirrored in our contemporary struggles. Issues such as racial equality, gender rights, freedom of expression, and technological privacy are at the forefront of today's legal battles. The principles established and contested in the cases within this book provide a foundation upon which we can build, offering guidance and insight as we navigate new and complex legal landscapes.

The legacy of these historical verdicts lies not only in their immediate outcomes but in their enduring influence on our collective conscience. They remind us that the law is a living entity, evolving with society and reflective of our highest aspirations and deepest flaws. It is through the continual examination and re-examination of these landmark cases that we can strive to create a more just and equitable world.

In closing, "The Historical Verdicts: Pivotal Court Cases Through History" invites you, the reader, to carry forward the insights gained from these trials. Let them inspire you to engage critically with the legal and moral questions of our time, to advocate for justice in all its forms, and to contribute to the ongoing dialogue that shapes our shared destiny. The pursuit of justice is an unending journey, and each of us has a role to play in ensuring that the scales are balanced for generations to come.

The End.